The FIRST BASEMAN

The FIRST BASEMAN

Baseball
Behind the Seams

TOM KEEGAN

CINCINNATI, OHIO

The FIRST BASEMAN
Baseball Behind the Seams

EMMIS BOOKS
1700 Madison Road
Cincinnati, Ohio 45206
www.emmisbooks.com

Edited by Jack Heffron
Cover and Interior Designed by Stephen Sullivan
Production Design by Carie Adams

Cover Photo by Elsa/Getty Images
Back Cover Photo by Transcendental Graphics

DEDICATION

This book is dedicated to John R. Keegan, oldest and wisest of my nine siblings and a big-time basher of corny book dedications.

ACKNOWLEDGMENTS

Thanks to Dolph C. Simons Jr. for enabling me to delay the start of my exciting new job as sports editor of the *Lawrence Journal-World* so that I could finish this book. Thanks to Sean Casey, Ken Griffey Jr., Jerry Narron, and Rob Butcher of the Cincinnati Reds for being so generous with their time. Special thanks to Reds shortstop Felipe Lopez for repeatedly letting me sit in his chair to interview Sean Casey. Thanks to Kathy's House in Wauwatosa, Wisconsin, the hospitality house where I lost a best-of-three Battleship series to my brother John by the slimmest of margins. Thanks to wife Angie, children John, Andy, Jimmy, and Ellen, and dog Sammy, the six biggest reasons I go to bed every night looking forward to tomorrow. Thanks to *Rocky Mountain News* baseball writer extraordinaire Jack Etkin for introducing me to Rockies first base coach Dave Collins, one of baseball's hidden treasures. My gratitude goes out to *San Diego Union-Tribune* columnist Tim Sullivan for recommending me for this project and to Jack Heffron of Emmis Books for his patience. Kudos to forever-young friends Elden Auker and Bill Snead. And thank you Dwyane Wade for putting Marquette basketball back on the map to stay.

TABLE OF CONTENTS

Boston's Jimmie Foxx and New York's Lou Gehrig, two of the greatest first basemen ever, chat before a game in the 1930s.

1ST

Harder than it Looks

Leave it to *Seinfeld*, brilliance dressed in simple clothing, to capture the essence of the unflattering stereotype the first baseman battles daily for playing the Rodney Dangerfield of baseball positions. In an episode titled "The Boyfriend," Elaine, the sit-com's lead female character, is chatting up Keith Hernandez, who is playing himself.

> Hernandez: I hate to brag, but I did win eleven straight Gold Gloves. I wouldn't have brought it up, but since you mentioned it.
>
> Elaine: I didn't mention it.
>
> Hernandez: Well, I won them anyway.
>
> Elaine: Well, so what? I mean, you played first base. I mean, they always put the worst player on first base.

She couldn't have uttered more hurtful words if she spoke for days than with that one cutting exchange. For decades, the stereotype of the first baseman was that he was fat and lumbering, more closely resembling a beer league softball player than a major leaguer. The stereotype painted the first baseman as a statue who stands there and catches what is thrown right into his oversized mitt and does little else but come to the plate every couple of innings to swing for the fences.

Hernandez, now an insightful, candid color commentator, took that stereotype and crushed it farther into oblivion than Frank Howard ever belted a home run. Hernandez did it with nimble feet and mind, with a pro-active approach that belied the notion the first baseman waits for the plays to find him. You know the stereotype, the one that says if you can't run, can't throw, and swing too lethal a bat to sit and watch, grab a first baseman's glove and just keep working on that swing, Slugger.

"That's one of the greatest fallacies in baseball," Hernandez says of the stereotype. "The first baseman is involved in more plays than anybody but the catcher."

Other players, less graceful and experienced at a position that still doesn't earn the respect it deserves, echo Hernandez's sentiments.

Based on interviews done in the summer of 2005 during a whirlwind tour of several big league ballparks, herein we will explore how the position is more difficult than it appears, and delve into other aspects of first base, such as:

- Toughest play: Probably any kind of backhand. You've got to go down the line, you have to throw almost a hook shot. It's hard to get around. That ball that really drags you into foul territory.

- The conversations that take place between base

runner and fielder, coach and even umpire, which make first base the most social of all positions.

- The advantages—some obvious, others far more subtle—of being a left-handed first baseman.
- A day in the life of a major leaguer, Sean Casey, who also happens to be baseball's friendliest player and chattiest first baseman. It's in that stretch shortly before the game, when he doesn't say a word, that he reveals his inner self, the one that makes him such a compelling figure.
- Pointers on how to play the position from experts such as Don Mattingly and Keith Hernandez, two men who owned two different segments of New York City at the same time.
- A man who learned from scratch as a professional how to play catcher, then late in his career was eaten alive by first base. Mike Piazza makes it clear he wants nothing to do with the position ever again.
- A look at the triumphs and sufferings of Hall of Fame first basemen Jimmie Foxx, Lou Gehrig, and Hank Greenberg through the eyes of the last lucid link to a bygone baseball era, their friend Elden Auker, a submarine-style pitcher who teamed with two of them and faced the other.

The tour begins at Yankee Stadium, where the Tampa Bay Devil Rays are in town and manager Lou Piniella, embattled by a miniscule payroll and a grossly inexperienced roster, takes a moment from the daily grind of trying to pretend he enjoys managing a roster slightly too good for Triple A and not nearly good enough for the major leagues.

Piniella isn't seated behind his desk in the cramped visiting manager's office. Rather, he's seated against the wall, tying his shoes.

"I played [first base] some at the end of my career," he says. "No, thanks. Not for me. There's a lot more to it than you think. And I'll tell you one thing that might surprise you. When you first get over there, you wouldn't believe how quickly that pickoff throw from the pitcher gets over there. That really takes some getting used to."

Doug Pensinger/Getty Images Sport/Getty Images

LOU PINIELLA

Piniella's failure to master first base isn't why he took his frustration out on first base. It was umpires' calls that made him dig the bag loose and hurl it into the air, earning him *SportsCenter* time and suspensions.

"I've only done it twice," Piniella says, smiling at the memory. "Once in Cincinnati. Once in Seattle. The first time I had a little trouble getting it out of the ground. The second time it came out easy. The third time? There won't be a third time. If I tried to do it now, I'd throw my back out."

Out the manager's office, through the clubhouse, out

the door, a left turn into the empty hallway, a quick right turn up the empty tunnel, a left turn into the dugout, and there sits a man who has inherited the mantle from retired Sparky Anderson as baseball's pre-eminent storyteller. Don Zimmer seldom is without a baseball bat. He cups his left hand over the handle and occasionally pounds the bat onto the dugout floor. Put in a quarter— he's been around the game long enough to remember when it was only a penny—and out comes a great baseball story. This is a more gentle Zimmer who sits beside me than the one I remember from that day in the visiting manager's office at Dodger Stadium in 1990, the one who stood nose-to-nose with me and hollered, "Maybe if you didn't stay out so late you could keep your head up, watch the game, and not ask such a stupid question!" He had an amazing radar that way when I covered him as a beat writer for the now defunct *National Sports Daily*. He always knew I closely watched the game on a given day. Maybe he measured the bags under my eyes. Maybe he gauged the conviction in my voice when I asked the questions. Whatever it was, he was regularly right on target. He's not the manager now and in fact isn't even allowed to sit in the dugout during games, so he sits in the stands once the game starts.

I put my quarter in the slot by telling Zim, "I never knew there was so much to playing first base until I watched Mike Piazza try to do it."

His right hand—the one that break dances while he's watching a horse race on which he has a vested interest, the index and middle fingers rubbing furiously against the thumb—comes off the bat, and the left hand stays on it as he gently taps the dugout floor. His mind races back.

"Little more to it than you think," Zimmer starts. "I was managing my first year for Knoxville. Ran out of players, so I called up to Cincinnati, and I told Chief Bender, 'Chief, I need you to send me another player.' He said, 'I ain't got none. Can you play?' I said, 'No, I can't play.' Well, I had to. I had no choice. So I say to myself, 'What position can I play where I won't get injured?' I says, 'I'll put myself at first base.' Well, there's a grounder to third base, and Bernie Carbo was playing third base. His throw is wild, up the right field line. So I try to go up the right field line to get it and still keep my foot on first base. The runner run me clear into right field. I called time and told the right fielder, 'You come in here and play first base. I'm going out to right.' Little more to playing first base than you think."

Off to Chicago and Wrigley Field, where Zimmer held his most high-profile managing job. The Cubs are in the midst of another season that would not meet expectations, though first baseman Derrek Lee can't share in the blame. He is on his way to a remarkable season with the bat and glove. At season's end he wins the Gold Glove, his second, as well as the National League batting title. He also leads the league in hits, total bases, slugging percentage, and OPS, and finishes second in home runs. But mostly because of his team's poor record, he finishes third in the MVP voting behind Cardinals first baseman Albert Pujols and Braves outfielder Andruw Jones.

The notion that it matters little which batsman is

Jonathan Daniel/Getty Images Sport/Getty Images

DERREK LEE

handed a glove and pointed to first base is shattered easily by studying the defensive statistical data of Cubs third baseman Aramis Ramirez. Before he made his throws across the diamond to the tall, agile Lee, Ramirez committed 33 errors in 159 games at third base with the Pirates and Cubs in 2003. In 2004, his first season teaming with Lee, Ramirez committed 10 errors in 144 games at third base.

"Right now, Derrick Lee is the best player in baseball," Ramirez says. "Offensively, yes, people talk about that, but nobody talks about his defense. He's a Gold Glover. When you get a guy like that, you just catch the ball and throw it. Just worry about catching the ball and throw it over there. When you throw it over there, somehow he's going to catch it."

The best player in baseball? That simply isn't said about Lee, yet if he were as superior defensively to the more productive offensive peer at any other infield position, he would certainly be considered a contender for the best player in baseball. Albert Pujols usually puts up even better offensive numbers but doesn't save nearly as many errors as Lee, who finished 2005 batting .335 with 46 home runs, 107 RBIs, 120 runs scored and 50 doubles.

Asked if he enjoyed hitting or fielding more, Lee couldn't make up his mind.

"Both," Lee says. "I take pride in the whole game. I don't think one is more important than the other. I really enjoy defense. When I'm on defense, I enjoy that. The toughest play for me is probably the double play, being right-handed and having to throw across your body. The first baseman's main job is to save errors, pick balls out of the dirt, make plays around the bag. It's one of those things where it goes unnoticed when you're saving errors. You can save your team a lot of errors and it saves runs. I played third my first year in the minors. I think they switched me because I got a little too big. When you're 6'5", you're normally going to get switched to first base because they don't want to waste that big a target."

Lee's production at the plate is such now that a manager would find a place for him in the lineup, even if he were a defensive liability, instead of a Gold Glove fielder. That place, however, wouldn't necessarily be first base.

Off to Cincinnati, up in the media dining room at Great American Ballpark, home of the ever-struggling Reds. Several baseball generations after he told Zimmer he couldn't send him a player, Chief Bender quietly eats dinner and enjoys a chuckle over the relaying of the Zimmer tale. A few tables away, a pair of scouts discuss the dangers of putting any old statue at first base.

Jim Fregosi, once traded for Nolan Ryan and four other players, is noted for having one of the sharper minds in the game of baseball. His success as a manager suggests he should be managing somewhere, but since the explosion of salary inflation, general managers steadily have gained more power with owners, who feel more comfortable letting men who dress like them, talk like them, and hold cocktails like them, with napkins wrapped just so around the glass, handle their money. General managers tend to feel threatened by men as opinionated and smart as Fregosi. Before the opener of a series against the Colorado Rockies, Fergosi is chatting with highly regarded Dave Yocum, a scout whose evaluations passed along to GM Kenny Williams, helped to shape the 2005 World Champion Chicago White Sox.

"Bobby Knopp was at second base, and I was at short," Fregosi says, harkening back to his days as a young hotshot with the California Angels. "You've heard of Tinkers to Evers to Chance? When Dick Stuart was playing first base, Bobby and I used to say Tinkers to Evers to take a chance."

Today, Dick Stuart, aka Dr. Strangeglove, would be in the American League.

Let's suppose Lee, instead of having a Gold Glove had a stone one, where would he play if he stayed in the National League?

"Ideally, I think you can get away with a mediocre third baseman over a first baseman," Fregosi says the way he says everything, with absolute conviction. "The first baseman handles more balls than anyone but the catcher. Everyone thinks anybody can play first base and that's not true. Defensively, how many games are saved by a good defensive first baseman? Infielders are more comfortable throwing a ball to him. If I had a guy over there who can really catch the ball, it really relaxed the infield. The first baseman makes or breaks his other infielders. Travis Lee, between [utility infielder Jorge] Cantu and [shortstop Julio] Lugo, I can't tell you how many errors he's saved."

Chimes in Yocum: "I'll tell you something else that's changed—guys bounce throws to first base now. Guys didn't used to throw when a ball was hit deep in the hole. They'd eat it. Now they bounce throws over there, especially with AstroTurf, so the first baseman has to make more tough plays than he used to make."

Fregosi adds: "And with a first baseman that has any range, you can set your whole defense a different way. A lot of guys stand three steps from the bag, and the first thing they do is run to the bag when the ball is hit. Balls go through all the time. I've seen so many bad first basemen cost so many games."

Downstairs, hours before first pitch, Reds manager Jerry Narron is one more day closer to having the interim removed from his title by making players more accountable and more mindful of the details that when executed can enable a team with less talented players to play better than the team with better players. Narron was a catcher most of his playing career and played some first.

"A lot of people think anyone can play it, and that's just not the case," Narron says. "There are a lot of nuances of playing first base that a lot of guys just can't pick up on. In this league, there are so many more bunt plays, which makes it even tougher to play first here than in the other league. A lot of guys have trouble with throws up the line, where guys have got to come off the bag and catch the ball. Some guys are afraid of the runner running into them when they come off the bag. It's not as easy as it looks. Another tough one is that little in-between ball. When I was over in Boston, making out the lineup card for Grady [Little] and Kevin Millar was at first base, I put a little "4" next to his name because he was going after everything. He'd catch a ball in front of Todd Walker, and

Brian Bahr/Getty Images Sport/Getty Images

TODD HELTON

there'd be no one over there at first to catch the throw."

In the home clubhouse, Casey, Narron's first baseman, is asked to cite the toughest play.

"Probably the double-play ball," he says. "As a right-handed thrower, you have to make the pivot and then throw, and it's such a bang-bang play."

Lee gives the same answer in Chicago and so does Jim Thome in Philadelphia from his seat in the spacious home clubhouse packed with all the modern amenities of an elite country club.

The answer to the same question draws a greater variety of responses for left-handed first basemen.

Says Rockies first baseman Todd Helton: "Probably coming off the bag with a left-handed hitter at the plate. Third base is the hot corner, but they get to stand still, whereas we're shuffling off the bag. Your head's moving and that makes it harder to pick up the ball."

At Yankee Stadium, hitting coach and former first baseman Don Mattingly offers another perspective: "The toughest play is probably any kind of backhand. That ball that really drags you into foul territory, you have to throw a hook shot almost."

The first baseman makes the highlight package by making a diving stab, getting up on his knees, and tossing underhand to the pitcher covering the bag. But that's not the play that makes the first baseman's night.

"The biggest thing a first baseman does is pick up his teammates by picking up bad throws and making outs," says Helton from the seat in front of his locker. "You make an error and you're down on yourself the rest of the game. You can really pick up a player and help the team that way. That's one of the great things about playing first base, being able to pick up your teammates."

He said it's one of the great things. He didn't say it was the greatest.

"The single best thing about playing first base is the short run to the dugout," Helton says. "About five steps."

In making those five steps, Helton leaves behind conversations with the opponents for conversations with his teammates.

Don Mattingly on the Intricacies of First Base

Love the Yankees or hate them and you have something in common with half the sporting public. No matter on which side your loyalties lie, there's no denying when it comes to baseball nicknames, nobody does it better than the Yankees.

With the exception of well-traveled closer Jose Mesa, whose moniker is the English translation of his name (Joe Table), the two best baseball nicknames in recent history are Yankees legends: "The Boss" and "Donnie Baseball".

DON MATTINGLY

Of course The Boss is George Steinbrenner. Just look at his gait—so slow, so over-the-top in its side-to-side movement. Check out his attire: If he weren't The Boss someone would have the guts to tell him that turtlenecks in the dead of a muggy summer weren't even good fashion when turtlenecks were the rage. Who else makes a big production of saying goodbye to the employees to make sure they all know he is leaving the premises, ambles to the parking lot, drives his car around the block once, and returns to work so that he can catch his workers with their feet up? If he's not The Boss, then why has pitching guru Billy Connors for decades now sat next to him in all the show-of-hands meetings, waiting to see whether Steinbrenner raises his hand or leaves it at his side, then does the same, forever voting the same way?

Why can't the Yankees players grow beards and wear long, straggly hair? Because The Boss says so, that's why. From his ever-pointing finger to his authoritative voice, everything about the man screams The Boss. The handle is such a great fit, nearly as great, even, as Donnie Baseball.

There have been greater Yankees than Don Mattingly, the greatest Yankee never to win a World Series. There never has been another who defined his sport quite so perfectly. Think about the great Yankees and something about their celebrity comes to mind. Babe Ruth was larger than life, so naturally he was bigger than baseball. Think of the Babe and you think of the grin, the odd-shaped body, the fun-loving ways off the field, the outrageous power at the plate and at the gate. Charisma. Celebrity.

Think of Joe DiMaggio and before long you think handsome, you think Marilyn Monroe, you think Mr. Coffee.

The name Lou Gehrig, unfortunately, arouses images of pain and suffering and premature death, the trappings of the disease that bears his name, the disease that starts to attack the nervous system and never stops.

Mickey Mantle? Speed, power, and sadly, excessive carousing that led to an early death.

Yogi Berra? You think 10 World Series rings, then you think cartoon character, then you think wild sayings delivered in fractured English: "It ain't over till it's over... When you get to the fork in the road, take it. ... Nobody goes there anymore. It's too crowded."

Reggie Jackson? You think REGGIE! So does he.

Derek Jeter? You think man about town. If he hadn't dated the starlets—Mariah Carey, etc.—you may think differently, but he did, and there's no turning back. The gossip columns fanned those flames, and now it's part of Jeter's image.

Don Mattingly? You think baseball. Period.

The Yankees unveiled a plaque for Mattingly in Monument Park on August 31, 1997, and on that day Mattingly uttered the quote that best summed him up.

"I always wanted to keep it strictly baseball," he said during a press conference. "When the fans thought about me, they thought about baseball, not about a commercial or about a celebrity or anything like that."

Speaking into a microphone, Mattingly expressed similar sentiments to the 55,707 who packed Yankee Stadium on that first Sunday of the 1997 NFL season: "I tried to keep it pure. I tried to keep it simple. I tried to play great baseball for you over the years."

Tried and succeeded.

The film clip that best captures the blue-collar, down-to-earth Mattingly's connection with the fans—they always considered him one of them—came during the Yankees lean years, when he chased an out-of-reach foul ball to the edge of the stands and came away with a mouthful of popcorn.

"It was one of those foul balls that was six, seven rows back that you can't reach, but it's high and you kind of get there," Mattingly recalls. "So everybody's looking at the ball. Nobody's looking at me. The kid's got the popcorn there. And he's staring at me. I said, 'Can I have some of that?' He was just looking at me with his mouth open and couldn't say anything. So I snatched some. I sent him an autographed ball the next inning and signed it, 'Thanks for the popcorn.' I guess he did some news shows after that. That's the kind of thing that was news then because we weren't winning any games. That was big news."

Mattingly's sarcasm was on target: The Yankees were not a good team then and it was not big news. It was a small gesture that perfectly captured Mattingly's friendly spirit and demonstrated he appreciates the impact ballplayers have on children. His numbers were big, his stardom bigger, indirectly because he never courted fame, never came off the slightest bit phony.

A bad back shortened Mattingly's prime, kept him out of the Hall of Fame, denied him the torque he once had and thus stripped him of his once considerable power. He had so much clutch in him though that he was able to say farewell to his millions of supporters with a turn-back-the-clock performance in his only postseason experience, the five-game series against the Seattle Mariners in 1995.

He hit .417 with five extra-base hits and six RBIs.

Such a series would have done to a ballplayer what par on the 18th hole does to so many of us hopeless hackers who keep coming back, convinced the key to the mystery that is the golf swing finally has been discovered. For Mattingly, the key to his swing was lifting his leg, which he did the final couple months of his career, bringing about a rebirth that culminated in his terrorizing the Mariners only to fall short in the epic series. No matter, Donnie Baseball had made up his mind his family needed him to come home to Evansville, Indiana, so home he went.

Ten seasons later, Mattingly, hitting coach for the Yankees, is busy darting from here to there in the Yankees' clubhouse, preparing for a Sunday afternoon series finale against the California, er, Anaheim, check that, Los Angeles Angels of Anaheim. We agree he'll find me when he has a window in his schedule to talk about the art of playing first base.

It's obvious he's going to be awhile, so a long walk down the corridor to the visiting clubhouse won't risk losing access to Mattingly.

Angels manager Mike Scioscia is always worth visiting, always worth interviewing on any baseball topic. As a player, Scioscia didn't have much power at the plate for a man his size, but nobody blocked the plate better, framed pitches more skillfully, or guided a pitching staff with more leadership than Hall of Fame manager Tommy Lasorda's favorite catcher.

"Mike Scioscia, toughest man in baseball!" Lasorda

was fond of bellowing. "Not only that, he's Italian."

Lasorda forever lobbied his organization to groom Scioscia to become the sort of long-term Dodgers manager that he and Walter Alston were. He never made it out of the minor leagues with the Dodgers as a manager, because the organization had gotten too arrogant, too corporate to listen to the likes of Lasorda. After all, why listen to a man who managed the Dodgers to two World Championships? Why listen to a man who was such a skilled communicator he managed to purge the insecurities of young ballplayers so completely that nine, count 'em, nine of Lasorda's players were named National League Rookie of the Year?

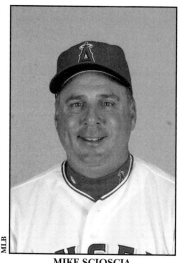

MIKE SCIOSCIA

Scioscia went on to manage the cross-town Angels to the 2002 World Championship, and the Dodgers, who have not been back to the World Series under any of Lasorda's successors as manager, have been picking eggshells out of their eyebrows ever since.

Scioscia and Angels coach Mickey Hatcher, close friends since their days as teammates with the Dodgers, both were unlikely home run heroes during a memorable run to the 1988 World Championship. They've won a lot of games together. That success could partially explain why neither man is burdened by that common baseball malady: insecurity. They have equally thick skin, particularly when throwing barbs each other's way.

"What are you talking to Mickey for?" Scioscia says. "He doesn't even know where first base is."

Hatcher's retort: "When Mike played first base, they didn't need a second baseman. He was so big he covered the whole right side himself."

On the contrary, when Scioscia played first base at the end of his career after his arm fizzled, he covered little ground and evoked memories of what a good catcher he was. He did his best, just as he does when asked a baseball question.

The topic: What are the biggest advantages left-handed first basemen have over right-handed throwers?

"You lose a little to the line as a left-handed first baseman, but where you're worried about is not as much the line as the hole, especially when you're holding the runner on," Scioscia says. "The hole can get really big with a right-handed first baseman who doesn't have range. He just gets off by a step and now that hole is so big you could roll a ball through there. As a left-handed first baseman, you've got coverage, you've got the angle on the hole. And coming in and fielding bunts and throwing to any base is easier. I think there are functional advantages to being left-handed. Guys knew that when they started to lay out the game more than a hundred years ago. Same with a catcher being right-handed. When you're throwing to the lead base, third base is easier, that's probably the biggest reason catchers are right-handed. Most hitters were right-handed when they first started the game. They didn't realize you could swing the bat left-handed when they first started playing the game so it was easier to throw to second for a right-handed catcher. There are some great defensive first basemen who throw right-handed, but there are definitely some built-in advantages to being left-handed."

The best defensive first basemen while Scioscia was playing were both left-handed: Keith Hernandez and Mattingly. The time had come to return to the Yankees' clubhouse to check Mattingly's availability. The clubhouse, at the moment, has 25 empty lockers and a room full of reporters who are talking to each other, wishing they had players to interview. Access to the coaches' room is denied to reporters in the Yankees' clubhouse. After a short wait, Mattingly walks down the hall from the room where the coaches dress and into the clubhouse to fulfill his promise of an interview.

"Let's do it over here," Mattingly says when that time comes, "so I can spit into the garbage can."

Chewing tobacco. To most of the outside world, it's a disgusting, dangerous habit. Different rules apply in this universe. It's simply part of what makes him Donnie Baseball.

Standing next to him, the first thing that strikes you is that he's not a tall man, wasn't a big target. Then as the conversation thickens, and he begins to demonstrate footwork that had him covering so much ground in every direction without leaving the imaginary base, you realize he was a huge target. He was something of a Baryshnikov of the bag. At the age of 44, he still showed such remarkable flexibility, balance, and harmony between baseball mind and body. It's easy to forget what freaks of nature professional athletes are, because they compete against other freaks. Somehow, watching him stretch in each direction with such body control brought it home more than watching him play games.

Listening to him talk with such nonchalance about throwing both left-handed and right-handed, depending on the position he played, in his early teen years served as another reminder that though Mattingly is a regular guy, he's a very special athlete.

"I played first base early," he remembers. "I played everywhere, but even in Little League, I played a lot of first base. I could throw both ways. In the Civic League, I'd catch, play short, and play third, and throw right-handed at those positions. I was still dominantly stronger left-handed, but I could throw naturally both ways, and I did up until I was 13, 14 years old."

And one more time, when playing for pay as a minor leaguer, Mattingly slipped on the right-handed infielder's glove. It was during his first Instructional League.

"I was playing around right-handed, catching balls at second base, and turning double plays," he recalls. "Mickey Vernon came up to me and said, 'Get rid of the glove.' I said, 'What are you talking about?' He said, 'They see that, they'll make a utility player out of you. Get rid of the glove.' "

So ended Mattingly's right-handed baseball career. No regrets.

Mattingly was taken in the 19th round of the draft out of Reitz Memorial High School in Evansville, Indiana, where legend has it he did not swing at and miss a single pitch during his senior year. Mattingly spent much of his minor league career as an outfielder. Darryl Strawberry, who more than a decade later would become his teammate with the '95 Yankees, had a hand in Mattingly becoming a permanent first baseman.

Asked to name the hitters who smashed the hottest balls down the line, Mattingly didn't need much time to come up with an answer.

"Freddy Lynn came down there hard consistently," Mattingly responds. "And Straw. In spring training you always knew if he got one, it was going to be a rocket. Straw got me over there to first base. We were in St. Pete, and I was playing right field. Remember when they were trying everybody at first? Well, that day they were trying Roy Smalley over at first. Straw hit a freaking pea rod at Smalley. I mean a rocket. Nobody catches that ball. I'm in right field, and it was cuffing me. The next day I'm playing first."

Nine Gold Gloves later, Mattingly had cemented himself as the greatest defensive first baseman in Yankees history. So where does he start when teaching the position to young athletes? The same place Joe Pepitone started with him.

"Feet," Mattingly says. "Feet are the most important thing. You've got to learn to get to the ball in the right spot. If the feet are good, you get yourself a lot of good hops. Then from there you've got to really learn to get

Rich Pilling/Major League Baseball/Getty Images

DON MATTINGLY

the ball out of the glove, but the first thing I would teach is feet, getting into position. If the feet are working, it all falls into place. From there get the ball out of the glove. Then have your feet moving to the throw. That way you're automatic all the time. As soon as you catch it, the ball comes out and your feet are getting in position to throw to second base."

Pepitone had very disciplined feet around the bag, disciplined enough to win a pair of Gold Gloves. He didn't always have quite the same control of the rest of his body, as he readily admits in his autobiography, *Joe, You Coulda Made Us Proud.*

Pepitone, who quit the Yankees for several days in 1969 in protest of being fined $500 for leaving the dugout during a fight, had trouble curbing his voracious sexual appetite during his playing career. After his career ended, he found trouble of another sort—getting convicted on a drug charge. Many questioned his pencil on the golf course and others whispered behind his back about the authenticity of his mane.

To Mattingly, Pepitone was a great teacher and a friend. That's one of the beauties of the baseball industry. When it comes to fellow ballplayers, ballplayers don't have a judgmental bone in their bodies in regards to off-the-field issues. A ballplayer tends to evaluate a ballplayer on how he plays ball. Nobody could give Pepitone anything but straight A's as a defensive first baseman. Mattingly made Pepitone proud, learning the position so well the pupil surpassed the teacher in achievement.

"Peppy taught about moving my feet over there, using

the bag, how to go different ways off of it," Mattingly says with a grateful tone. And then he begins demonstrating footwork, exhibiting the elasticity of a rubber band, right there next to the garbage can in the Yankees' clubhouse.

"From first base, if you use your feet right, you should be able to go all the way this way, all the way that way, then back," he says. "There shouldn't be a ball from there to there if you have time. You shouldn't be able to catch and still be on the bag. It gets back to your feet. You've got to get squared up. A lot of guys on that double-play ball hit to short just kind of step out there. If I do that, now I'm stuck. Instead of getting here [squares up], and reading the ball before committing. I've got to read it and give myself another six, eight feet. That gets you in trouble a lot, stepping out. If I step out and anything gets behind me, I'm screwed. I get a ball that bounces, and I'm all tied up. I try to get guys to square up."

Now he's squared up and his eyes are the eyes of an athlete in the middle of a game. He's into it.

"It's kind of like guarding a guy in basketball," he continues. "If I'm here [squares up], I can go this way, I can go that way. I can block the ball in the dirt. I can go up if I have to. If I'm stuck here [stretching for the ball], I'm counting on a perfect throw or at least a good throw. You've got time. If you'll just read first, you'll make better plays."

Who else helped?

"Joe Altobelli," Mattingly says of the former Yankees coach who managed the Giants and Orioles. "Alto helped me by showing me to be on the line on the bunt. He always said you have to learn to play the line on the bunt. When I charge, instead of charging to the middle, stay down the line. That allowed me to go across the field with the ball and keep all my throws going that way, right to where I want to go. Basically I make every play to my right, so now I can come and attack. Everything's moving where I want to go, so it allows me to be a lot quicker and shorter."

Mattingly was the antithesis of the stereotypical big lug first baseman welded to the bag that he couldn't see because his belly got in the way.

"I like to play first like another infielder," Mattingly says. "I play deep. I play in the hole. I play in different spots all over the place. A lot of people stay around the bag. I was all over the place. J.T. [Snow] plays it like that. He's all over the place. Playing in the gap, playing deep. Keith [Hernandez] played it like another infielder. And Keith was really attacking on the bunt. He was unbelievable going to third base."

Like Snow and Hernandez, Mattingly had the advantage of being left-handed, which in his mind is no small edge.

"It's a tough right-hand position," Mattingly says. "Tino [Martinez] plays it unbelievable, but it's a pretty tough right-handed position. You've got to rotate on that throw to second. He's very good at that. He's outstanding."

Other advantages?

"The tag's not such a big deal," Mattingly says. "It's shorter, but not so much a big deal. All your plays are to the right mostly, so that throw's like a rhythm throw for a lefty. When you're right-handed you've got to get your feet all the way turned around. Playing this way [he demonstrates in the middle of the clubhouse] I can catch it and flip. If I've got my feet right, I can catch it and throw at the same time. I don't have to get turned around. It especially is an advantage on bunts. I go to third, bam. Second, bam. The angles are so much better. The right-hander's got to get turned around on everything. And it's a tough play when you have to get turned around and then throw. It's a lot tougher position right-handed, I think. It would be like trying to play third base left-handed. Everything's tougher because now on my throws to everywhere I have to turn."

Mattingly's left-handed, but he's as far from the flaky stereotype that so often in baseball triggers the saying, "typical lefty." He has an ability to keep things simple by fouling off distractions. That ability keeps him humble off the field, and it helped him keep his eye on the ball as a baseball player.

"It's not like he had great range," says Willie Randolph from behind his desk in the manager's office at Shea Stadium. "That's not what made him so good. He was pretty quick, he had a good first step, but he didn't have great range, most of the balls he got to he caught. He had very sure hands. He was always very focused. Playing defense is all about concentration and focus, and Donnie was as intense defensively as he was offensively. That's a big key. That's why you didn't see him make a lot of mistakes, because he was able to separate hitting from his defense. He was a real good hitter obviously, but he was able to separate it. That was never a problem for him because he is very focused."

The look on Randolph's face suggests he wishes Mattingly could bottle that focus and sprinkle it to the corners of the Mets' clubhouse where it's needed most.

WILLIE RANDOLPH

"A lot of players don't know how to separate their hitting from their defense," Randolph continues. "A lot of guys are out there hitting or just wandering out there [scans the ceiling with eyes rolled upward, mimicking that far-away look], thinking about anything. Mattingly was very, very focused and he took a lot of pride in his defense."

Randolph, so quick with his hands and feet, so adept at turning the double play, joined Mattingly to form one of the most efficient right sides of an infield to ever play the game.

"I know we were good together, and we had a nice little feel for each other," Randolph says. "There's always a very subtle chemistry between a first baseman and a second baseman, knowing where each other is, on the ball hit between you, when to go for the ball, when not to go for the ball."

I shared with Randolph a story Reds manager Jerry Narron (as mentioned in chapter one) told me about defensively challenged Red Sox first baseman Kevin Millar. As bench coach with the Red Sox, one of Narron's responsibilities was to transfer the lineup chosen by the manager onto the lineup card with a Sharpie pen. Narron said he used to write 4, symbolizing second base, next to Millar's name, instead of 3, because "he was going after everything. He'd always go in front of Todd Walker, and there would be no one over there at first base to catch the throw."

Smiling, Randolph points out, "I don't know why he'd do that. He wasn't going to catch the grounder anyway. Some first basemen know they're not good fielders and just go straight for the base."

Mattingly and Randolph didn't have any such problems.

"It's kind of a feel that you get, and Donnie and I had a nice little feel for each other," Randolph says. "I knew exactly where he was going to be, and he knew exactly where I was going to be. He knew my range. I knew pretty much what balls he would go after. It's like a double-play combination in a way, having that sort of sense where each other was on the field. A lot of players don't have that. A lot of players don't have that real feel for what balls to go for, what balls not to go for. It's almost like the first baseman feels like the second baseman has his back, and if he knows I've got his back, and if he knows he can't get a certain ball he'll just go straight to first. And he knows if I'm playing in a certain spot, mentally he knows he has to go for the ball."

Ballplayers like Randolph and Mattingly made

playing defense look easy. They had their routines down. Randolph played second base, though, so it's not as if he made it look so easy as to create the perception anyone can play there. Second is a position that commands more respect than that. First base, on the other hand, can be played by anybody, or so many believe.

To an extent, Mattingly buys into that.

"I really believe you can play anyone over there if they're willing to work at it," he says. "Even Mike Piazza, he can play first base if he'd be willing to say 'Okay, I'm going to play it.' Just basically be in the right position. Don't try to make the spectacular play. Just catch the ball that's at you. Learn to do the things I talked about with your feet. Don't try to be spectacular. Just catch the ball. Don't hurt your team. You can sacrifice defense there a little where a guy can still play it and not hurt your team. Not having to be spectacular. Just not hurt your team. Just be solid. That's what I talk to Jason [Giambi] about. Just be solid. Catch the balls you're supposed to catch. Make the plays you're supposed to make. Don't hurt your team."

I question whether Piazza could pick up the position, and I remind Mattingly that footwork has been the downfall of Piazza as a catcher.

"He could get it," Mattingly says. "It's a matter of making a commitment. There's no way that a guy is a big league player and can do the things he did and not be able to play it. I don't know if it's a case of if he's willing to try and to take time, but if he put in the time he could do it."

Piazza worked his way into the big leagues against long odds, but he was young and hungry then. Now he's an old dog by baseball standards. First base has more tricks to it than the average fan realizes. To play the position well requires a certain level of commitment. Mattingly seemed never to have a problem with that commitment to the position or to the game itself. Which is why his nickname always seemed to fit him like a glove.

A First Baseman's Timeline

July 18
1897

Transcendental Graphics

Cap Anson, first baseman for the Chicago Colts (soon to be the Cubs), earns his 3,000[th] hit, the first player to achieve that plateau.

August 5
1905

Hal Chase of the New York Highlanders, considered the best fielding first baseman of the deadball era, sets a major league record with 38 putouts in a double-header. In 1907 Chase makes 22 putouts in a single game, still tied for the record.

September 15
1902

Chicago Cubs first baseman **Frank Chance** completes the last leg of the legendary Tinker to Evers to Chance double-play combination for the first time.

Transcendental Graphics

October 9
1919

The Chicago White Sox lose the final game of the World Series to the Cincinnati Reds in what became known as the famous Black Sox Scandal. Sox first baseman **Chick Gandil** is said to be the ringleader of the crooked players.

September 3
1920

St. Louis Browns Hall of Famer **George Sisler**, records his 257th hit of the season, setting a major league record. Sisler won the MVP in 1922 and was elected to the Hall in 1939.

Transcendental Graphics

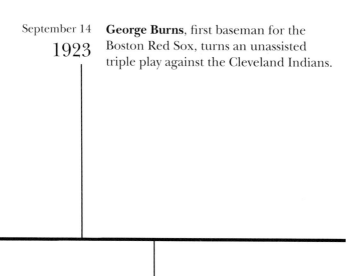

September 14
1923

George Burns, first baseman for the Boston Red Sox, turns an unassisted triple play against the Cleveland Indians.

June 2
1925

Wally Pipp, first baseman for the New York Yankees, asks for a day off, complaining of a headache. He is replaced by young Lou Gehrig, who will play 2,130 consecutive games before taking a day off.

Transcendental Graphics

July 6

1933

The first All-Star game is played at Comiskey Park. **Bill Terry** of the New York Giants starts at first base for the National League, while **Lou Gehrig** starts for the American League.

May 18

1934

Philadelphia Athletics first baseman **Jimmie Foxx** smashes a ball deep into the centerfield bleachers at Comiskey Park in Chicago, the first man to hit a ball that far in the old park.

1938 **Hank Greenberg** of the Detroit Tigers hits 58 home runs and was on course to break Babe Ruth's record of 60 until late in the season, when, according to rumors at the time, pitchers walked him intentionally to keep a Jewish man from breaking the record.

July 4

1939

Lou Gehrig Day is held at Yankee Stadium in commemoration of the greatest first baseman baseball has ever seen. His #4 jersey is the first to ever be retired in major league baseball.

47

1941

Rawlings introduces the first modern first baseman's glove, named the Rawlings trapper, made with three fingers and a deep well pocket.

July 1
1945

The first Jewish baseball player to win the MVP award, **Hank Greenberg**, hits a home run in his first game back after serving in Army.

Joe Adcock of the Milwaukee Braves hits a home run into the center-field bleachers at the Polo Grounds in New York, the first time it had been done in a major league game.

April 29

1953

1948

Transcendental Graphics

Johnny Mize, first baseman of the New York Giants, ties Pittsburgh's Ralph Kiner for the National League home run championship for the second year in a row. Both hit 40. In 1947 the pair hit 51.

Cincinnati Reds

1955

Cincinnati Reds first baseman **Ted Kluszewski** slugs 47 home runs and strikes out only 40 times. No player has accomplished this feat since.

Al Fenn/Time and Life Pictures/Getty Images

May 2

1954

Stan Musial, a lifetime St. Louis Cardinal and 3-time NL MVP, hits a record 5 home runs in a doubleheader against the Giants.

May 7
1956

NY Giants first baseman **Bill White** slugs a home run in his first major league at-bat. White goes on to become president of the National League.

1957

Gil Hodges of the Brooklyn Dodgers wins the first Gold Glove award for first base. He would win it again the following year for the National League while Vic Power of the Indians wins it in the American League.

National Baseball Hall of Fame Library/Major League Baseball/Getty Images

In the first game of his Rookie of the Year season, Giants first baseman **Orlando Cepeda** hits a home run, the first of 25 on the year. The "Baby Bull" went on to win the 1967 MVP.

April 15
1958

October 6
1963

In Game 4 of the World Series, with the score tied 1-1, Yankee first baseman **Joe Pepitone** lets a routine throw to first get by him, allowing the runner to advance to third and then score on a sacrifice fly. He made up for it the next year, hitting a grand slam against the Cardinals in Game 6.

July 6

1966

Boog Powell of the Baltimore Orioles drives in 11 runs, setting a double-header record, against the A's. Despite an 11-0 win in the first game, the Orioles drop the second 9-8.

July 24

1969

Phillies bad-boy **Dick Allen** is fined $2,500 for missing a doubleheader against the Mets. Stuck in traffic, the 1972 MVP was on his way back from the racetrack.

February 8

1972

National Baseball Hall of Fame Library/
Major League Baseball/Getty Images

Former Homestead Gray **Buck Leonard** is selected for the Hall of Fame, the only first baseman from the Negro leagues to be enshrined.

July 23

1974

Dodger's first baseman **Steve Garvey** wins the All-Star Game MVP, even though he was only elected through write-in votes. His .955 slugging average in All-Star games leads all with at least 20 at-bats.

Rich Pilling/Major League Baseball/Getty Images

Willie McCovey of the San Francisco Giants becomes the all-time leader in grand slams with 17. In the same game, he becomes the only player who has twice hit two home runs in an inning.

June 27
1977

November 13
1979

NL batting champ **Keith Hernandez**, who hit .344 for the season, and Pirates first baseman **Willie Stargell**, share MVP honors for the first time in history. Hernandez would add the hardware to his 11 straight Gold Gloves he won between 1978-1988.

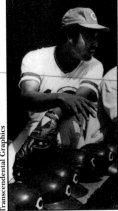

Transcendental Graphics

May 13
1985

With a pinch hit grand slam in the 7th inning of a game against the Phillies, Reds first baseman **Tony Perez** becomes the oldest man to hit a grand-slam in the 20th century, only to be surpassed by Carlton Fisk in 1991.

October 25
1986

With men on first and third, and with Boston only one out away from overcoming the "Curse of the Bambino" by taking the World Series, Red Sox first baseman **Bill Buckner** boots Mookie Wilson's soft groundball, and the Mets win the game and go on to win the series.

July 18
1987

Yankee first baseman **Don Mattingly** hits a home run in his eighth consecutive game, tying the major league record set by Dale Long in 1956.

August 2

1990

In just his 77th at bat, Yankee rookie first baseman **Kevin Maas** hits his 10th home run, the fastest anyone in league history to hit 10 home runs.

1997

White Sox slugger **Frank Thomas**, "The Big Hurt," becomes the first player in major league history to hit .300, hit more than 20 homers, and collect more than 100 walks, RBIs, and runs in 7 consecutive seasons.

September 8

1998

The Great Home Run Chase that brought the spotlight back to baseball culminates when St. Louis slugger **Mark McGwire** blasts his 62nd home run, becoming the first man to eclipse the 61 mark set by Yankee great, Roger Maris.

Elsa/Getty Images Sport/Getty Images

2003

May 11   Three-time Gold Glove first baseman **Rafael Palmeiro** hits his 500th home run of his career, becoming only the 19th player to join the exclusive 500 club. His use of performance-enhancing substances, which comes to light in 2005, tarnishes his otherwise brilliant career.

2005

Cardinals first baseman **Albert Pujols** is voted the National League MVP, leading his team to the Central Division championship and the NLCS.

4TH

A Day in the Life of a First Baseman— Sean Casey

His day is so typical for a boy of 12 years of age in Anytown, USA, typical, at least, in the days before video games replaced sweat and dirt. He wakes up, plays baseball with younger kids, breaks for meals, plays some more baseball with a mixture of older and younger kids, plays some more baseball with younger kids, breaks for another meal, watches some baseball on television, goes to bed and wakes up the next morning to repeat the daily ritual.

So what makes Sean Casey any different from so many baseball-obsessed pre-teens? For one thing, he's 31 years old. For another, his imagination doesn't have to create a public address announcer telling thousands of spectators his name and number each time he comes to bat, an echoing voice that triggers applause from thousands of passionate fans. And then there is the compensation, more than $6 million per season.

Sean Casey—the name just sounds like it belongs to a first baseman, doesn't it?—gets to live the dream and, get this, appears to appreciate just how cool a life that really is. He seems to relish every moment of it.

Baseball is a game of numbers and honors, league

leaders, and record-breakers. No such title for Nicest Man in Baseball exists. Unofficially, Casey inherited that mantle from Tony Gwynn when the Padres right fielder called it a career.

To spend a day with Casey is to realize his spirit has bathed in the fountain of youth. He remains 12, the absolute perfect baseball age: old enough to truly understand the game and its mind-expanding nuances, yet young enough to believe attaining major league stardom is possible.

It was 10:30 a.m. on Friday, July 15, 2005, in Mason, Ohio, two hours later than when Casey usually arises with his two sons. Andrew, 3, and Jacob, 2, leapt through the air and pounced on their father's bed to jump-start his day. The boys dragged their dad-child to the basement for some batting practice with a softball and a hardball bat. Sean threw overhand to Andrew and underhand to Jacob. He couldn't resist throwing one nasty curveball to Andrew, swing-and-a-miss, Strike 3!

Next on the agenda was a game of hide-and-seek, where the boys commanded their dad-child, "You be the bear! You be the bear!" The bear hid, the boys counted to 10, found the bear, the bear roared, the boys shrieked feigning great fear. Then the big boy and the two little boys went outside and dug in the dirt for a while. Two excited young neighbor girls spotted the Reds' first baseman, made their way over, and pleaded, "Can we have your autograph? Can we have your autograph, please?"

Casey obliged, signing baseball cards for them. Soon after that, Sean's wife arrived home from grocery

Andy Lyons/Getty Images Sport/Getty Images

SEAN CASEY

shopping and Sean made each of the boys a grilled cheese sandwich and fixed a tuna salad and a wrap for wife Mandi and himself. He put the boys down for a nap, and hung out chatting with Mandi.

Now it was time to make the 25-minute drive through at-times blinding rain to Great American Ballpark, the cozy ballpark in its third year of existence, the park that was supposed to be filled with former Big Red Machine fanatics and their children and grandchildren in the summer of '05. The moves new general manager Dan O'Brien made were supposed to juice a moribund franchise and breathe life back into a downtown that has lost its night buzz in the wake of riots in 2001. The best-laid plans backfired and not surprisingly Eric Milton, the left-handed flyball pitcher noted for surrendering home runs, the centerpiece of the winter reconstruction, has been a horrendous fit in the ballpark designed to take advantage of lefty swingers Ken Griffey Jr., Adam Dunn, and Casey.

A glance at the standings finds the Reds in last place in the National League Central Division. None of that seems to have tainted Casey's zest for his work and life in general. It is standard manners for a ballplayer to walk past someone he knows by name without acknowledging the person's presence. It's not considered rude, but it doesn't happen to be the way Casey goes through a day. On his way from the player parking lot to the Reds' country club-like clubhouse, Casey says hello to all the members of the security fleet and uses their first names: Roy, Kenny, Rickey, Bob, all the clubhouse attendants, anybody who crosses his path gets sprinkled with Casey's upbeat energy.

"I remember when I signed my contract four years ago for four years and $24.2 million, a lot of people around me said, 'You can get more, you can get more,' and I asked my dad what should I do," Casey says. "My dad said, 'Is it a livable wage?' I said, 'Yeah.' He said, 'Well, then sign it.' So I signed it. I always think whenever I see anybody, people have a job to do, a living to make to put food on the table. Me playing baseball is no different than what they're doing. They have talents that I don't have. I always make a point to say, 'Hey, how you doing?' All working class people should be recognized."

On this night, with the Colorado Rockies, cellar occupants of the National League West, in town, 21,116 would recognize Casey in each of his four trips to the plate, so the least he could do was prepare to the best of his ability in hopes of justifying their cheers.

After Casey says all his hellos and chats with several teammates, he accommodates an interview request because that's what he does when he gets reasonable requests. Professional athletes and executives generally fall into three categories in terms of media relations: the unreachable, the accessible but uncooperative, the cooperative.

Those who fall into the first group can be either hostile or distant. Former Cleveland Indians, Chicago White Sox, and Baltimore Orioles superstar Albert Belle is the poster child for this group. In what has to rank among the greatest sentences in sports writing history, Bob Verdi, then working for the *Chicago Tribune* once wrote, "Playing cards 3 feet from me in the White Sox clubhouse, Albert Belle could not be reached for comment."

Many executives fall into the second category. They can be reached for comment and will gladly talk all day long, the larger the circle of reporters gathered around them the better. They say nothing of value, reveal nothing, and therefore are uncooperative though they feel as if they have cooperated.

And then there are guys like Casey. They find the time to talk. They think about their responses instead of shifting into autopilot and spitting out a trail of platitudes. The topic is first base and all its nuances and Casey is happy to chat about it.

Question: What's the one play that everyone thinks is easy and it's really difficult?

"The pick," he says. "Picking the ball is not as easy as it looks. That in-betweener is really tough."

Later that night, Todd Helton would prove as much, failing to holding onto a dying, sinking throw from shortstop.

Question: What's the toughest play for you?

"Turning two as a right-handed first baseman," Casey responds without hesitation. "You're all over the place. You get it, turn, spin, throw, and get back to first. And you know what else?"

No, what?

"When the catcher throws down to try to pick off the runner, one of the weirdest plays is the blind tag," he says and then demonstrates what he's talking about. "You're trying to get the tag down. You don't know where the heck he is, and you're trying to get the tag down, you're feeling for him, and you're too late. Being a lefty first baseman would be great. I could see what's going on when the catcher throws down. Bam, you're right there and you can see what's going on."

Casey was the only one of several first basemen interviewed who said he had thought of that as one of the advantages of being left-handed and playing first base. It makes sense. When a left-handed first baseman turns his head in the direction of the glove, his head goes right to the spot where a successful tag can be made. If a right-handed first baseman were to turn his head in the direction of the glove, it would go to the inside of the bag, and all he could see is a safe runner's foot.

Question: There are two different philosophies on how to teach the same thing in so many different aspects of baseball. What is an example of two different philosophies of teaching a play to a first baseman?

Casey thinks for several seconds and then a light bulb that screams, "Oh, I got one!" goes off in his head.

"Coming off the bag," Casey says. "Sometimes, some guys say to give yourself as many feet as you can and come straight off the base. The other school is to get to the grass lip to take away those hops off the lip. In college, my coach always said you've got to get straight off the base and I always felt uncomfortable giving that lip away. Then one time I noticed J.T. Snow, one of the great first basemen, go to the lip. So I asked him, and he said he'd rather give up that extra foot or two than have to play a bad hop off the lip. He said he goes and gets the lip, and I was like, 'All right! If you think it's right, then it's right.' So I always get the lip."

That's the thing about so many aspects of baseball. There is no right way and wrong way. For example, former Yankee great Don Mattingly and current Cubs great Derrek Lee both said they play straight off the bag because that extra couple of feet can keep them in play for more balls.

Question: Besides picking wayward throws, what else about playing first base is taken for granted?

"You're getting some bullets over there," Casey says. "Left-handed pull hitters send some bullets your way. Cliff Floyd hits bullets. Jim Thome hits rockets. You're more like Eddie Belfour trying to pick it. Those big pull hitters. Man, it's no fun down there."

What else?

"Not just anyone can play first base," he says. "There's a lot going on. Stretching, there's a lot of stuff with footwork. Picks. When to pick, when not to pick. You're the cutoff man on balls to right-center and left-center. You're the double cutoff man on balls in the corner. The pickoffs at first. Knowing guys' moves. Bunt plays. When to come in. You're always getting throws. Every time a groundball is hit, even when it's not hit at you, you've got to catch the ball and that can mean making a pick, jumping to catch it and make a play. Sometimes it's treated like, 'Okay, you're playing first base tonight, here's a glove,' and guys don't know what they're doing.

They're stretching with the wrong foot. They don't get their footwork down. They don't get to the bag on time. A lot of times you'll see them say, 'We're going to make that catcher a first baseman.' They forget, when you're a first baseman, you're still an infielder. You've got to be athletic. You've got to know what to do with the ball. There's a rocket hit to you. Do you spin to it? Do you backhand it? Do you get rid of it? Do you get back to the base?"

Still, he's grateful he's a first baseman and not a catcher.

"The best thing is you don't have to squat," he says. "If I had to catch, my career would have lasted four innings, and I would have quit and gone home."

Go back far enough and you can find shortstop in the background of nearly every right-handed throwing major league ballplayer. Casey is no exception.

"I played short during the regular season, and when I played traveling all-stars they put me at first base," he recalls fondly. "I didn't think it was a demotion. I was just glad to be on the traveling all-star team. My coach would say reach out and touch someone, when I first played first base. And every time I go back to Pittsburgh, Dave Klasnick, my old coach, sits behind home plate, and that still sticks in my head. Bell Telephone, reach out and touch someone."

Others who helped him along the way?

"Johnny Goryl was an instructor with the Indians," Casey says. "He helped me out more than anybody. Sometimes, early on in college and at the beginning of pro ball, I had trouble throwing the ball. I was too conscious of bringing my hand back and was too mechanical. Johnny Goryl taught me when you make the play and you're down there stay down there. Flow through it and make the play. Take the angle down here [waist-high]. It sounded so weird at first, and I told him that. And he just told me that's how you do it, and I kept working at it and working at it. Now that's my strength, throwing the ball. I saw him this spring and went over and thanked him. Jay Bell came up with Cleveland, and when he won a Gold Glove he gave it to Johnny. He was always teaching me to go get the ball, be athletic."

He's not the only one to tell that to Casey.

"Barry Larkin used to say that, too," Casey says. "He'd say, 'Be an athlete, throw on the run,' when I used to take grounders with him at short. In college, it was always, left, right, left, get your arm out here. You're a robot. Being a robot helped me get fundamentally sound. Then I started looking at how guys did it. How they got the short hop. You have to be athletic, too. You can't just break it down all the time. You're going to have a ball hit to your left and you can't always get in front of it. You're going to have to make a backhand flip or something. Be athletic."

Casey also fondly remembers the mornings he spent with Indians instructor Brian Graham and fellow young first basemen Richie Sexson and Jim Thome.

"It was at 8 o'clock in the morning, before anyone was out there, the '98 camp, working with Brian for 20 minutes on picking balls out of the dirt and taking pickoff throws," he recalls with a smile. "I'd do eight picks, Richie would do eight picks, Jimmy would do eight picks, and we kept doing rounds like that. That's a great memory I'll always have. Every morning. All spring."

Casey has so much more to say but has run out of time. He has to join teammates in stretching exercises before taking batting practice.

With the first pitch of the 7:10 game two hours and a few minutes in the distance, Casey settles in for his first of three rounds of hitting. His first two swings are lazy, meant to achieve nothing but loosening his body and easing his mind into hitting mode. He then locks in and tries to go to left field with all the pitches, a couple of which were too far inside to achieve that goal.

"I'm just trying to get my swing going in that direction," he says.

After his final swing, he runs the bases, then spots a friend he visits behind the batting cage for a chat. As is the case with most men who talk with Casey, Rockies first baseman Todd Helton's body is shaking with laughter in no time. Until the 1990s there were rules against players from opposing teams fraternizing before a game. They had not been enforced for decades, but back in the day, an umpire would stand sentry during batting practice so that he could report any violators to the league office, which in turn would issue a fine to the offending players. The rule is off the books and the players briefly chat with friends in enemy colors without it hindering their pre-game preparation or dulling their desire to beat the bad guys.

Casey's plan is different for his second round of batting practice. Now he works on situational hitting.

"It's a hit-and-run, get-'em-over, get-'em-in round," he says. "Hit a sacrifice fly, and whatever other situations come up in games."

The next round he tries to "drive the ball where it's pitched. Right-center, left-center, just drive the ball."

For this round, he carries one basic thought beyond driving the ball: stay in the middle of the field. For the most part, he succeeds in doing so throughout the round.

His three rounds of batting practice behind him, Casey brings his glove to first base and through simple hand signals lets the coach hitting him grounders know what he wants to work on.

Not quite 20 minutes after taking his first hacks in the batting cage, Casey takes his first grounders. As with his hitting, he takes it slow at the beginning then ramps it up.

"At the beginning I'm just getting loose," he says. "The first four or five are right at me. Then I tell whoever's hitting to give me five to my left, five to my right, then I take 10 balls that I throw to second."

Players generally enjoy batting practice and Casey, not surprisingly, seems to be having a good time.

"I like my whole routine," he says. "Not just hitting. I enjoy taking grounders too. I always enjoy hitting the most. Any time as a boy you enjoy hitting. I look at my kids. They love to hit too. You throw them the ball they just want to hit something. Whether it's the ball, the couch, your head, they just want to hit something."

David Maxwell/Getty Images Sport/Getty Images

SEAN CASEY

Look at what Casey's sons have fun doing, and you have a window to what turns on Casey. The boy in him never is tough to find.

After the Reds finish batting practice and vacate the field so the Rockies can do the same, Casey retires to the clubhouse to make himself a light pre-game snack. On this night as most nights, it's a small tuna salad.

Eating gives Casey a rare break from his favorite pastime: talking. Before, during, and after the game, the garrulous first baseman seldom stops flapping, except for a half-hour pre-game period of silence he considers a key to his success on the field and in staying grounded outside the game.

Baseball plays subtle games on the head and slowly batters the body throughout the course of a 162-game season. Kirk Gibson, World Series hero of the '84 Tigers and '88 Dodgers, always has called a baseball season The Beast. Baseball is a kid's game, but when it's played by the most mentally and physically skilled practitioners of the sport, it can make a grown man feel as helpless as a baby.

To tame The Beast requires harnessing the highs and keeping the lows at bay. A hot hitter tends to become too eager to swing the bat, his front shoulder flies open, his head doesn't stay on the ball, and his body doesn't stay back long enough. The pumping adrenaline brings about the end of the hot streak when the hitter begins to get himself out.

The slumping hitter gets too down on himself, begins to overanalyze his hitting mechanics, listens to too many coaches and teammates for advice, and doesn't trust his hands to do the work. As veteran baseball writer and youth baseball coach Kevin Kernan is fond of saying, "If you think, you stink."

A game of failure, baseball preys on the inevitable insecurities that creep into a player's head. The late Tim Crews, who died in a spring training boating accident while with the Indians, was among the friendliest ballplayers in the game. He was an open book whose insecurities were on display daily, providing a nice case study of just what The Beast can do to a man's psyche.

One look at Crews during his days as a reliever for the Dodgers in the late '80s was all that was needed to determine how his last outing went. If the smile on the face of the mustachioed reliever reached from just below one ear lobe to just below the other, his last outing was successful, his question asked of me predictable.

"Do you think they're going to trade me to a contender in August?" Crews would ask, smiling. "Some team that needs a closer? Come on, I know you know something but you're sworn to secrecy. That's okay. I respect that. But as soon as you can tell me, let me know. Come on, you can tell me now, can't you?"

Crews didn't have the God-given ability to close games for a major league team, but his adrenaline pumped so mightily after the good outings he convinced himself he was a hot commodity. And he became too confident on the mound, too daring with hitters, which led to a bad outing.

If the bounce from his step was gone, the smile late in forming, and the head was hanging, Crews' last outing was a bad one and his question for me was markedly different: "What are you hearing? Do you think they're going to send me to Albuquerque? You haven't heard anything like that, have you?"

If it was a particularly bad outing, it tended to cause other bad outings, because Crews would then become too careful and fall behind hitters.

In getting too keyed up over good performances and too down after the bad ones, Crews was not alone. Rare is the player who can maintain that flat emotional line. Rare is a Derek Jeter, whose robotic mindset results in robotic performances.

Off the field, the fame ballplayers attain can swell their heads to the point they begin to think their brilliance extends beyond the baseball diamond. Too many can surround themselves with hero worshipers and believe the nonsense showered upon them. While working their way into the ballplayer's favor, the hero worshipers also convince the player that anyone outside his inner circle is not to be trusted. The result: the ballplayer can become a suspicious, self-important, unfriendly person.

With all these forces at work, staying grounded is not an easy thing to accomplish, especially for someone with as hyperactive a brain as Casey.

As a player and a person, Casey has done a marvelous job of remaining down to earth, and he gives part of the credit to his 30 minutes of silence.

On this evening as on all others when game time is approaching, Casey grabs a couple of books from his locker, excuses himself, explains he's heading for the chapel, and in the process he reveals he's something of a mind-reader by saying, "And I'm not going there to pray for hits," he says.

Sure, he's not.

"No, really, I'm not," he says.

So what is he doing? He's reading Mother Theresa books. On this day, the two he reads are *The Joy in Living* and *A Simple Path*. Casey never tires of reading the same passages.

"I've been doing it my whole career," Casey says. "The times I've gotten away from doing it are the times I've struggled. It helps me relax and helps me get away by myself."

Tension is a side effect of The Beast, it can make a hitter strangle the bat and can cause a pitcher to grip the baseball too tightly. It can squeeze every last drop of joy out of the game. To relieve stress is to tame The Beast, at least temporarily.

"For some reason, it kind of brings me to a peaceful feeling," he says. "Humility. One of the things [Mother Theresa] says is that when you're humble neither praise nor disgrace can touch you. When people say you're the best, you're really not. When people say you're a piece of crap, you're really not either. Nothing can touch you. because you know what you are. It's about knowing what you are."

Casey, raised Catholic, doesn't turn his faith into a shaving cream pie in the face, yet he is comfortable talking about it. Athletes who play for what derisively is referred to as the God Squad so often become judgmental, thereby going directly against the teachings of their religion. Casey isn't ashamed of his deep faith, but knows he plays for the Reds and is not a God Squad player.

"In my life and in my faith I really believe God's in control and that if I look to people and see His love in everybody and find a good thing in everybody it's easier to live life than to go around bashing everybody, being negative about everything, or think that you're better than somebody else or think that you're worse than somebody else," he says.

He fumbles through a book and finds the exact quote that gets him ready for game time daily and reads it aloud: "If you are humble nothing will touch you, neither praise nor disgrace because you know what you are. If you are blamed you will not be discouraged and if they call you a saint you will not put yourself on a pedestal."

Now that his mind is in game mode, Casey, a compulsive stretcher throughout the day, puts the finishing touches on his body. At 6:50, he leaves the chapel and heads for the tunnel behind the dugout, where he gets his juices flowing with "probably 10 sprints."

The lineup card posted on the Reds' dugout wall shows a line that reads: "3. 21 Casey 3." He's batting third, wears number 21, and plays first base. Since Casey is a native of Pittsburgh, most assume he wears number 21 to honor late Hall of Famer Roberto Clemente, whose rifle arm, unconventional hitting form, arms-flying-all-over-the-place running style, and clutch 1971 World Series performance made him the Pirates' most popular player.

As a boy, Casey's favorite player was left-handed-hitting first baseman Will Clark, whose best years were played with the San Francisco Giants. Casey wanted to wear Clark's number 22 in the minors, but teammate Wayne Hoyt already had it. He was assigned number 20. When he got to the majors, that wasn't an option. The Reds retired number 20 in honor of Hall of Fame right fielder Frank Robinson, who hit 586 career home runs in an era long before steroids inflated home run totals beyond recognition.

Casey isn't the classic number 3 hitter Robinson was, because, though he makes consistent contact and is an efficient situational hitter as was Robinson, he is not blessed with great power. This power shortage also sets Casey apart in a negative way from most men who play his position. Perhaps, if Casey weren't emboldened by the words of Mother Theresa, this shortcoming would eat away at his psyche, drive him into funks, maybe even drive him all the way out of the game. Who knows? Mother Theresa is not alone in giving Casey the strength to keep his lack of power from eroding his confidence. Spoken words, from the mouth of veteran first baseman John Olerud, entered Casey's left ear, during a conversation at first base, and lodged in his brain forever.

"John Olerud had some great years in Toronto, and then he struggled, and he told me the reason he struggled was they wanted him to be a home run hitter," Casey says. "He hit .250, .260, trying to be a home run hitter. He told me to just be who you are. Don't let anyone change your approach. Be who you are, and the rest will take care of itself."

Who Casey was coming into this game is a .313 hitter with 20 doubles and just three home runs. For a player with a 3 in front of his name and behind it on the lineup card to also have a 3 under the HR category on the statistic sheet in mid-July is extraordinary. The fact none of them have come at home run-friendly, lefty-tailored Great American Ballpark boggles the mind, though not Casey's mind. Know what you are. Casey knows what he is not: a home run hitter. He is a contact hitter who sprays line drives to all fields. He is not an easy man to strike out and is about a month removed from a streak in which he went 73 consecutive plate appearances without a strikeout. His .305 Reds career average places him in the top 10 all-time among Reds who played in at least 500 games.

Batting in front of a resurgent Ken Griffey Jr. has enabled Casey to see good pitches to hit.

Griffey and Casey are in their sixth season as Reds teammates, and it's easy to see they are close. Griffey has needed friends, given all the speedbumps and bruises he's encountered during a homecoming that set the town ablaze with anticipation of a second coming of the Big Red Machine when Jr. was acquired by the Reds in February of 2000. The city of Cincinnati celebrated the arrival of the game's brightest star with a fireworks display.

His first season with the hometown team went well. He hit 40 home runs, drove in 118 runs and scored 100. He was healthy enough to play in 145 games. Then as if the baseball gods were trying to balance the scales of a career that made Griffey the Barry Bonds (with a better throwing arm) of the American League during his 11 seasons with the Mariners, he averaged less than 80 games over the next four seasons. He checked onto the disabled list seven times with serious injuries to his left hamstring, right knee, right hamstring, right shoulder, right ankle, right hamstring again, and right hamstring one more time.

The complete tear of his right hamstring was so disabling that Griffey had three screws inserted in surgery.

The screws attach the tendon to the bone. During all the breakdowns, Griffey's spirits went the way of his body. He seemed depressed, especially when he believed his desire to play the game he was raised in was questioned.

I've chatted with Griffey a few times through the decades and left each conversation wanting him to do well, even on those occasions when he seemed distant, suspicious, curt. Even then, his devotion to the game came through.

On this evening, before the opener of the three-game series with the Rockies, Griffey is particularly friendly. He follows me into the hall outside the Reds' clubhouse, says hello, and polls every teammate who strolls past with the same question: "Who's the most talkative first baseman in the game?"

The same answer, given with an expression that screams "Isn't it obvious?" rolls off the tongue of all of them: "Sean Casey."

Griffey uses the term "great guy" more than once of Casey. And then he chats about his favorite topic: His children. Talking about his three kids' athletic preferences and skills seems to have the same effect on Griffey as reading about Mother Theresa has on Casey. It puts him in a relaxed frame of mind, makes him appreciate that he's still a kid when he's between the lines, playing the game he's healthy enough to play again.

Trey, 11, still plays baseball at his father's behest, but football is his passion. He's a running back whose style calls to mind Eric Dickerson, according to his father, in part because "he's so much taller than all the other kids." Her father won't be surprised if Taryn, 9, one day goes straight from high school to the WNBA, a league she already studies intently, particularly her hometown Orlando franchise. Tevin, 3, already is baseball-obsessed.

Casey has the ability to put a positive spin on just about anything, but watching Griffey go through the injuries and the accompanying criticism hasn't been easy.

"He's one of the best players ever," Casey says. "And as good a player as he is, he's that good a guy too. The rap he caught was so unfair. He was hurt, and people were questioning his character. That's what bothered him."

Nothing seems to be bothering Griffey on this night. He and Casey are healthy and ready to take their best hacks at Rockies right-hander Jason Jennings, opposed by Reds righty Aaron Harang. Dale Scott is the home plate umpire, Tim Tschida's working first base, Ron Kulpa's at second, and Dan Iassogna is at third.

Casey tosses grounders to the other infielders, and then after Harang tosses his first pitch at 7:12 p.m. of what would be another efficient night for the tall, thick right-hander who pitches a baseball far better than he swings a bat, Casey begins what would be an evening of nearly non-stop conversation. He first engages first base coach Dave Collins, a good friend from Collins's two years as a coach with the Reds.

The first-inning conversation that took place between pitches, as recounted by Casey and Collins, was about Todd Helton, who spent the opening months of the season in the biggest slump of his career, went along these lines:

DAVE COLLINS

Casey: "How's Helton doing? It looks like he's swinging the bat a little better."

Collins: "Much better."

Casey: "What's the biggest change he made?"

Collins: "His confidence is back."

Casey: "What left him that came back?"

Collins: "I don't think anything left him. Just his confidence came back. He'd gone longer than he'd ever gone without hitting, and I think that once he started to get some hits his confidence came back. And since his confidence has come back he's been more aggressive."

Casey: "He's a gamer, isn't he?"

Collins: "Yes, he is. He plays the game the way it's supposed to be played. He's a superstar who still keeps the game first and his individual self second. He's kind of like another guy I know, wears No. 21 for the Reds."

Casey laughed, but as Collins says later, "He knew I was serious."

Harang pitched a 1-2-3 first and Felipe Lopez, Rich Aurilia, and Casey were prepared to baptize Jennings, who took a 5-8 record and 5.24 ERA into the night.

Lopez led off with a single up the middle, bringing Aurilia to the plate and Casey to the on-deck circle.

On many nights, particularly on the road, a spectator seated within earshot of the hitter on deck will holler: "Hey, Casey at the bat."

To which Casey has a standard response: "Hey, that's pretty original. Never heard that one before."

He punctuates the retort with a laugh so rich it could warm the heart of an assassin. The momentarily embarrassed fan is left with a smile on his face and a story to tell his buddies.

Lopez takes second on Aurilia's grounder to third and Casey, who had driven in only two runs in the previous 14 games, has himself a prime RBI opportunity.

Casey never is at the bat without his trusty shin-guard.

"I fouled a couple of balls off my shin a couple of years ago, and I couldn't walk, so I thought I got to get a guard," he explains. "It never hits the shin-guard though.

It hits my leg, it hits my toe, it hits everywhere now, but never the guard."

(Less than a week later, Casey was sidelined after fouling a ball off his foot).

Casey sets his back foot in the batter's box and pulls his right foot back while he unfastens and refastens his batting glove, a ritual he repeats before every pitch.

"If I'm still thinking about something I'll do it again," he says of the glove ritual. "I do it pretty quick. Boom, boom, boom and I'm usually ready before the pitcher is ready to throw his next pitch."

Jennings delivers a sinkerball that flirts with the southern border of the strike zone. Casey views it as a little low and takes the pitch. Scott calls Strike 1. Casey unfastens and refastens his glove and settles back in.

Casey explains what thoughts were percolating at this point: "Jennings has a good changeup, and he likes to throw it. I was thinking I was going to try to get a ball down. He threw me a changeup and I got just enough of it to get it over Helton's head. Good thing Derrek Lee wasn't over there. He might have had that."

Lopez scores from second, and the Reds take a 1-0 lead.

Up next is Griffey, who runs a full count, which has Casey running with the pitch. Griffey fouls off two consecutive 3-2 pitches and Casey chugs back to first, breathing heavily. If ever he is tempted to dog it in such situations or getting out of the box on what looks like a sure out, the words of Collins, his old pal, echo in his brain: "If you can't give your team four seconds four times you shouldn't be allowed to put on a big league uniform. You're not mentally tough enough to handle flying out to center, so you're going to run half speed to first base? Give four seconds to your team, or give up your paycheck."

Casey runs hard on each Griffey foul ball, but that doesn't mean he can't gripe about it in good fun: "He's been killing me all year fouling off so many pitches."

On the next pitch, Casey's running isn't for naught as he takes second base on Griffey's grounder to first. Joe Randa strikes out swinging to strand Casey at second.

Casey and Collins resume chatting in the bottom of the second, this time centering on the starting pitchers. First they talk about Harang, National League Pitcher of the Month for May, who but for the Reds' anemic offense would have better than the 4-8 record he took to the mound for the start.

Collins: "What kind of makeup does Harang have? He looks like a tough kid."

Casey: "He's all business. He's a man."

They then discuss how impressed they were with Jennings' competitive nature.

The Rockies drew just two walks for the game and three of their six hits were for extra bases, so it was a relatively quiet night for Casey in terms of chats with opposing baserunners.

The score still is 1-0 Reds when Casey is at the bat for the second time against Jennings, again with one out and Lopez on second base, this time in the third inning.

Casey takes Ball 1, then swings at a well-placed Jennings cutter that veers in on Casey's hands and jams him for a popup to center field. Jennings got Casey out with a good pitch, rather than Casey getting himself out, an at-bat Casey can put behind him without regret. After Griffey walks intentionally, Randa lines out to center to strand Lopez.

Helton leads off the top of the fourth for the Rockies and falls behind, fouling off Harang's first two pitches. Before the third pitch, Casey shifts a couple of steps toward the line after studying catcher Jason LaRue giving the signs to Harang.

"Helton's just such a good hitter he can keep balls fair," Casey explains. "I saw LaRue called for a fastball in, and he was really in off the plate, so I knew if he was going to miss he was going to miss really in or in off the plate. Helton's only way to keep it fair was going to be down the line. I do that a lot, depending who's up. I might not do that if a little slap hitter was up, because he maybe doesn't get to that ball."

Helton gets to the pitch, and just as Casey figured, rips it over the bag. Casey stabs the hot shot and takes it to the bag for the out. More than just Reds players and fans are grateful Casey's head was in the game. If not for Casey gloving the hot shot, the ball might have bruised the first base umpire in a most painful way.

"You saved my life," Tschida tell Casey. "You saved my life."

Casey: "That's right. You owe me one, brother. You

owe me one. I saved your life."

It's a debt on which Casey knows he'll never collect.

Thanks in part to Casey stealing a double from Helton, Harang completes his third 1-2-3 inning, and the Reds go three up and three down in the bottom of the fourth. The Rockies tie it 1-1 in the fifth after Jorge Piedra lead off with a double and scores on Danny Ardoin's one-out single to center.

The top of the sixth features the game's first dispute with an umpire. Aaron Miles leads off for the Rockies and is upset when Scott does not award him first base. Miles maintains Harang hit him with a pitch. When it becomes apparent the argument will not end any time soon, Casey leaves his position and walks over to Tschida to initiate a conversation.

Surely, Casey must have been asking how difficult a play it is to call when a batter is grazed by a pitch, or claims to be anyway, right, Sean? Wrong.

Casey recounts the conversation that took place on both teams' first game back after the All-Star break:

Casey: "So what did you do during the break?"

Tschida: "It was unbelievable. I had a five-day break. I smoked six cigars in five days."

Casey: "That sounds great. Did you fly in today?"

Tschida: "Yeah, I flew in today."

Casey: "I think I gained four or five pounds over the break. I was eating so much pizza and a bunch of junk."

Tschida: "Yeah, I must have gained like eight pounds, drinking all the wine I drank."

The argument breaks up at the plate, and Casey strolls back to his position. Harang makes his way through his fourth 1-2-3 inning of the night.

Casey, leading off the sixth, takes a pair of balls for a hitter's count and tags an outside pitch that shortstop Luis Gonzalez snares for a hard lineout. Griffey follows by nailing Jennings' first pitch well beyond the right field fence to give the Reds a 2-1 lead, which was where the score would stay until the bottom of the eighth.

By then, Casey and Collins have engaged in conversations about numerous topics, including new manager Jerry Narron, who is in his 20th game since taking over for fired Dave Miley.

Collins recounts the conversation:

Collins: "Are things better than they had been?"

Casey: "They are."

Collins: "What's Jerry like as a manager?"

Casey: "He treats us like professionals."

Collins: "That's good because you are a professional, and you get the treatment you deserve. If you act like a pro, you should get treated like one. And if you don't, you shouldn't."

The Reds take a 2-1 lead into the eighth and to this point in the game the standouts have been Harang, who left after seven innings of one-run, three-hit, one-walk ball, and Griffey, who not only hit the go-ahead home run, but went back so gracefully, breaking with the crack of the bat, on a ball hit to the edge of the warning track in the early innings. Griffey was about to make his biggest

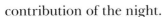

contribution of the night.

Facing Reds reliever Matt Belisle, pinch hitter Eddy Garabito draws a one-out walk and takes second base on Cory Sullivan's groundout. Aaron Miles strokes a single to center and most in the house believes the game is about to be tied. Griffey charges the ball and unloads it quickly, firing a perfect throw to LaRue in time to nail the speedy Garabito on the game's pivotal play and preserve the 2-1 lead.

Casey leads off the bottom of the eighth intent on reaching base to give the Reds' bullpen a cushion. Reliever Bobby Seay starts the inning for the Rockies and delivers two fastballs on the outside corner to get ahead of Casey, who keeps the bat on his shoulder for both pitches.

"It wasn't what I was looking for," he said afterward.

Casey takes two more pitches, both balls, to get even in the count and then gets a hitter's pitch … and did nothing with it. He grounds weakly to short.

"He threw one right there for me, and I was just kind of feeling for it instead of letting it rip," Casey says. "That's the one at-bat I'd like to have back. I was a little too defensive. Otherwise, I felt good. I felt like I showed up all night defensively, and I felt like hitting I showed up, too, other than that last at-bat."

Those who study counts and analyze hitters' tendencies will tell you hitters who start behind in the count and arrive at a 2-2 count fare worse than those who start ahead in the count and fall back to 2-2. Casey, in analyzing his final at bat, provided a window into a hitter's psyche that helps to explain the statistical tendency. Once a hitter lapses into a defensive mode during an at-bat, it's difficult to shift out of it. If a hitter falls from ahead to an even count, he subconsciously tends to believe it's his turn to regain the advantage in the confrontation with the pitcher.

Casey's at-bat doesn't derail the Reds and apparently doesn't fuel Seay's confidence. Griffey follows with a five-pitch walk, and Adam Dunn sends Seay's final pitch way over the fence in right-center to give the Reds a 4-1 lead for closer David Weathers to preserve.

As the ninth inning starts, Collins, an exceptional baserunner in his day, is still fuming from the game's pivotal play, Griffey throwing out Garabito at the plate to deny him the tying run in the top of the eighth.

Collins recounts the conversation he had with Casey, who is nowhere near as fast as Garabito:

Collins: "Sean, do you score on that ball?"

Casey: "Yeah, I do."

Collins: "That's right you do. And the reason you score is you get a real aggressive secondary lead, and you're anticipating moving on the strike. You're not as fast as he is, but you made up for it with your preparation before the pitch. And that's what separates a contender from a pretender."

Pitch.

Collins: "Do you run the catcher over there?"

Casey: "Yeah, I do."

Pitch.

Collins: "That's the way you play the game. You play it because you love to play the game. You play it to win and you play it for keeps. That's the way you play the game."

And that's why Casey is among Collins' favorites.

"If you don't like Sean Casey, you don't like human beings," Collins says. "He's one of the most genuine, down-to-earth, enthusiastic, and, one of the most important words, *grateful* people I've met. I love him. He's just an incredible person. I pull for him. He deserves everything he gets."

Still, he wears enemy colors. No matter how close two men within the baseball fraternity are, the uniform trumps friendship every time once a game begins. That's why Collins felt not the least bit guilty about the lie he told Casey during the game that night, a lie he revealed the next day.

"After a runner takes off on a steal, very often the first baseman will ask me, 'Was that a hit and run or was that a straight steal?' Normally, I tell him the opposite," Collins says. "Last night Casey asked me was that a hit and run? I told him no, that was a steal. It was really a hit and run. He thinks I think he was just making conversation. I know he was trying to get our signs, but he doesn't know I know that. Now he thinks he's got our hit-and-run sign."

Collins won that game-within-a-game that could benefit the Rockies down the road, but on this night Casey's team won the game.

The Reds' 33rd consecutive day in last place ends not only with a victory, but with a reminder of how even the wins don't come easily for a team so flawed. Piedra tags

Weathers for a two-run home run to make it 4-3 before Weathers strikes out Gonzalez for the final out to get credit for the, ahem, save.

Afterward, the manager's office is alive with talk of Griffey's resurrection.

"He's trying to make the All-Century team in two centuries," Narron says. "Did you see the blood on his pant leg? I think he switched pants during the game. There's a little Roy Hobbs stuff going on here."

The gash in Griffey's leg is from the hamstring surgery that hasn't completely closed, Casey explains, and at times "it oozes blood, and this nasty puss," and stains his pant leg. Griffey sparkled on defense throughout the three-game series and homered in each game to push his career total to 521, his season total to 20 in his 84th game, remarkable considering his first didn't come until April 30.

"Remember the big thing on ESPN at the end of April was: 'Is Griffey ever gonna hit another homer?' Now look at him," Casey marvels after the game.

Casey hasn't showered yet because though the game is over there is more play time, more swings in the indoor cage, though he's doing the pitching, not the hitting.

Andrew and Jacob, who had watched the game with their mother in their seats in the family section, are eager to finish their days the way they started them, hitting their favorite pitcher.

At one point, Andrew declares, "I don't want to share the bat anymore. I'm not sharing."

Daddy: "Okay, then if you don't share, then you can't

hit."

A panicked Andrew: "Okay, okay, I'll share, I'll share."

And so he shares. After the postgame hitting, the boys take a ride home from their mother and Casey grabs a quick postgame meal in the clubhouse: world-famous ribs from the Montgomery Inn. Soaked with sweat and the odd drip of rib sauce, Casey is badly in need of a shower. He takes a long one in the clubhouse, gets back into his casual summer clothes, heads for the players' parking lot, and drives home.

"I wish I could just go home and go to sleep right away, but I can't," Casey explains. "I'm too wired. I don't get to sleep until 1 or 1:30."

So he stays up and watches television. Watching *Baseball Tonight* on ESPN is part of his nightly ritual.

The next day he recounts a conversation he had with Mandi as he was watching *Baseball Tonight*.

"Don't you ever get tired of baseball?" Mandi asks.

Pause to reflect on the question with an expression that suggests the question is as foreign to him as if it had been asked in Russian.

"No," the husband answers his wife. "Not really."

Think about it: Sean Casey tired of baseball?

Since when does a 12-year-old boy blessed with the right physical and mental tools to excel at the national pastime ever grow tired of baseball?

5TH

Keith Hernandez and His Innovations

A sk any first baseman who played the position in
the major leagues during the past twenty-five years
to name the man who played it best, and the majority
will give the same response and give it quickly: Keith
Hernandez. He played it better than the rest physically,
mentally, and vocally. By watching him play, fans—and
even other players—could understand the intricacies
of the position better than before. Kids just starting out
could learn what was possible. Hernandez personified
the position not only as it should be played but as it could
be played.

I had an idea how to express generally how he
changed the position and told him so and also told him
that before sharing that with him, I wanted to get his
impression of how he changed the position.

"How I changed the position," he echoed, his wheels,
as always, turning a million miles an hour. "I don't know.
To me it's just plain old baseball, but I guess there were a
lot of things I did that a lot of guys didn't do. You never
see a second baseman throw out a runner going to third
base. I would always throw out a runner going to third,
particularly if it was a slow runner with nobody out and

the guy at the plate is trying to advance the runner."

Okay, Keith, a nice start. How else did you change the way the position is played?

"The bunt, I guess," he said. "But that was all just Cardinals stuff, fixed timing plays with the pitcher. That's what I brought over from the Cardinals to the Mets. I knew when the pitcher was going to come over and when he wasn't. He keyed off me, and I was able to get that other step."

Players routinely marvel at how aggressively Hernandez attacked bunts and gunned out the lead runner. Hernandez wasn't expansive on his answers initially, and I had a suspicion as to why. He wanted to hear an outsider's view on how he changed the position and since I had planted that seed, he quickly asked for the answer.

I told him: "First base was considered a reactive position until you came along and turned it into a proactive one."

He paused.

"I never heard it put that way," Hernandez said. "Proactive. I like that word. That works. I played it aggressively. That's the way I was taught. I was always trying to get the lead runner. There are ways to be proactive in rundowns."

Such as? Now, without intending to, Hernandez was about to reveal his brilliance, about to illustrate how a curious mind, exceptional visual systems, and natural-born leadership qualities enabled him to go where no first baseman had gone before him.

"If it's a rundown between first and third, by sending the runner at first on a steal attempt to get caught in a rundown so the runner on third could score, we had great communication on that play," he said. "I had it with Tommy Herr with the Cardinals and Wally [Backman] and [Tim] Tueffel with the Mets. I realized the second baseman and the shortstop can't see the runner at third. They have the ball and they're running the runner back to the base, and I don't want them worrying about the runner. One day, I realized I don't have to look directly at the runner. I could look at the shortstop position and see the runner out of the corner of my eye. With my head between second and third, I could see both runners. There's a certain point, he gets too far down the line, if he's twenty feet off the bag, and the shortstop or second baseman is running back to me, I gave them a hand signal and a verbal signal to let them know. If the runner broke home, I'd say "home." If the runner got out too far, I'd run right toward the runner at third, get him in a pickle, point and say "run him" or "third." Three different commands. I'd always get that runner in a situation with the shortstop and the third baseman coming back to me because that runner now thinks he has a chance. He now knows the shortstop and the third baseman can't see him."

In other words, he baited the runner into breaking for home, when in fact the same move that baited the runner to break for home was the move that signaled the fielders to throw home. By watching Hernandez play the position as nobody played it before or since, we could see the attributes that made him so good: Great visual systems, which also enabled him to recognize pitches so well, played a part in him reading the ball so well off the bat. Quick reflexes gave him that first movement in the right direction the instant the ball was read. Superior flexibility enabled him to contort his body in such a way as to make plays on balls that seemed destined to be extra-base hits. A passion for playing the game gave him the desire to figure out a way to become involved in plays that weren't normally considered part of a first baseman's job description.

That passion triggered a mind that was able to create ways to get involved. And there was one more trait Hernandez brought to the job that gave him the confidence to go where no first baseman had gone before him. He has a voice that cuts through the din and into the right ears. His voice carries, and if not for that God-given ability, he wouldn't have been able to take charge quite the way he did.

"I could scream in front of 40,000 people, and they could hear me," Hernandez said. "Darryl [Strawberry] could hear me in right field. I just had a voice that carried, They heard me. I loved to do that, and that was the fun part of the game. If you can make a difference and you're involved, that's fun."

Hernandez doesn't claim to have been perfect. Baseball is too complicated a game, too physically and mentally demanding, to ever attain perfection at any aspect of it. He doesn't claim to have mastered every responsibility that goes with a first baseman's job description.

"My one deficiency was I was never really good at cutoffs," Hernandez said. "You don't want to rush this throw. A lot of times I would get a bad grip on the ball out of the glove. It didn't happen too much in my career because as a first baseman you really aren't involved too often—only on a base hit to right field or center field. The ball in the gap, the second baseman or the shortstop is going to throw it in. Even though you're the second cutoff man, you're not going to cut their ball off."

There was one other thing Hernandez wasn't very good at: Doing nothing, even if the book said that on certain plays the first baseman can pretty much take the play off and catch his breath.

For example: "Sometimes on the ball hit down the right field line, the second baseman goes out as the relay man and the shortstop stays on second base. If no one is on base, I really don't have much to do but watch the runner to make sure he tags first base. On that play there is really no one to tell the second baseman what to do. Is it an automatic double or could it be a triple? So I try to make myself useful and tell him where to throw it, whether to hold it or throw to third. It's either do that or stand there twiddling your thumbs, and I never much liked twiddling my thumbs."

Twiddling his thumbs—another Hernandez deficiency because he lacked experience at it.

Enough about his deficiencies. Hernandez played far ahead of the pack in so many ways, and he has his proactive mind to thank for much of it. He had a knack for making

KEITH HERNANDEZ

even the difficult play look easy. Pitchers appreciated how he fed them on plays he made that left him too far from the bag to get the out without the pitcher's assistance.

"I would always want to get it to him before he gets to the bag so he didn't have to worry about catching the ball and stepping on the bag at the same time," Hernandez said. "It looks easy throwing it to the pitcher covering the bag, but if I'm in the hole that's about a thirty-foot throw, or if I'm way in the hole, that's about a fifty-foot throw. Wherever I was, wherever my eyes were, it would click in my head to throw it ten feet ahead, and that was a perfect lead. That was just something I learned through experience. It looks easy, but it can be a long throw and it gets a little more dicey when Vince Coleman, Ozzie Smith, or Willie McGee is coming down the line. It's a bang-bang play then. And it's all the more dicey if there are two outs with runners on base, and they're going to score if you screw it up."

In the case of Hernandez, that's a mighty big if. Nobody played the position better than he played it. Even if he were right-handed, he would have been a perennial Gold Glove contender, but Hernandez is grateful he was born left-handed. For all the reasons detailed by Mattingly, Casey, and others in previous chapters, Hernandez considers the right-handed first baseman to be at a great disadvantage.

"I would not have been a very good third baseman," Hernandez said. "And it's the same with right-handed throwers playing first base. Right-handers can play it, but if it's going to be played to perfection, it has to be

played by a left-hander. A right-hander can play it to near perfection, but a great fielding right-handed first baseman will never play it as well as a great fielding left-hander."

Interestingly, when asked to name the best defensive first baseman he saw, Hernandez mentioned Mattingly, just as Mattingly mentioned Hernandez. No surprise either way, but it was how they mentioned each other—with that reverential tone each used when talking about the other—that revealed the level of mutual respect.

"Mattingly played it very well," Hernandez said. "Mattingly should have been over in our league. He would have fielded so many more bunts, would have had more chances to show his skills."

After Mattingly, Hernandez mentioned a number of other masters of the position.

"Mark Grace," Hernandez said. "I liked the way Mark Grace played the position. Andres Galarraga has to be in the mix. Will Clark was good, but he could have been a much better first baseman than he was. Will was too Fancy Dan, too stylish. He had a chance to be really good, but he had a little mustard on him. I had some mustard too, but I had the basic fundamentals."

Hernandez also went above and beyond the job description to help teammates play winning baseball. Things such as, "letting the cutoff guy in front of you that you're trailing, letting him know where the ball is going to be thrown, instead of sitting on your ass and doing nothing. There are ways to get involved. First base is one of the least boring positions. No one gets more activity other than the catcher in the course of the game. That was the fun part of the game, being involved without cutting in on someone else's territory."

Wait a minute, Keith, you mean you can't just hand a first baseman's glove to the big, strong home run hitter who can't run and can't throw and can't play anywhere else, point him to first base and tell him to catch what's thrown to him?

"That's one of the biggest fallacies ever," Hernandez said. "If you've got a butcher over there, a Dr. Strangeglove, he's going to lose a lot of games for you. No one gets more opportunities in a game than a catcher and a first baseman. Infielders, when they're making their throws, have to be confident that when they're throwing to you, you're going to be able to scoop it. If you can't scoop the ball, it's down the right field line. There are a whole lot of things that are going on for an infielder to make a tough play, and if worrying about you scooping the ball is in the back of their mind when they've got to make a play, and the game's on the line, and there's no margin for error, and the ball is hit in the hole, and Vince Coleman's running, and you've got to come up firing, you can't be worrying about making the perfect throw. You're making the throw on the double-play ball, and you know you're going to get taken out, you can't worry about making the perfect throw. You've got enough to worry about just getting rid of the ball."

Turning errant throws into outs and verbally communicating were far from the only ways Hernandez made teammates better defensive players. Los Angeles

Angels of Anaheim—rolls off the tongue, doesn't it?—
manager Mike Scioscia played on a Dodgers team that
had many knock-down drag-outs with Hernandez's Mets,
the most memorable being the 1988 National League
Championship Series won by the Dodgers in seven
games.

"Keith Hernandez was the best I saw," Scioscia said.
"And not just because he was so great getting the lead
runner on bunt plays all the time. Keith was a difference-
maker defensively. The whole infield was better. He made
Wally Backman so much better. Wally Backman couldn't
go to his right, but he could make the play on the ball up
the middle because he didn't have to go to his right. He
could play there. Keith Hernandez had so much range
he had the hole covered, and Wally didn't have to worry
about it. And the 3-6-3, 3-6-1 double plays, nobody did
those quicker than Keith Hernandez."

So it's no wonder Hernandez loathes the stereotype
of first base being the hiding place for a bad glove. In fact,
the only time he didn't mind it was when it was spoken to
him on *Seinfeld*, as discussed in the first chapter.

"All I cared about was whether I was going to
remember my lines," Hernandez said of his experience
filming the television show. "The baseball jargon, those
were the easy lines to remember."

6TH

Mike Piazza, the Butcher of Flushing

The 65-mile drive up Interstate 5 in June of 1988 wasn't exactly the old-school baseball scout's idea of an efficient way to spend his precious time, not when the destination held so little promise and the potential for so much uncomfortable baggage.

Dodgers scout Gib Bodet asked himself, "Why me?" as he settled in behind the wheel of his home away from home, a 1986 Toyota, the vehicle that facilitated his search for diamonds in the rough, sometimes even on rough diamonds more suited for rock-throwing than baseball. Bodet put 150,000 miles on the car in three years, before giving it to his wife, Jean, who would put no more than 1,000 miles on it over the next 15 years. Therein lies the source of such wickedly high divorce rates among baseball scouts. The scout is forever in his car on the way to the next ballgame. The wife is forever at home, so often doing the job of both mother and father.

The first day of kindergarten, Little League Opening Day, learning to ride a bicycle—these are the events in a child's life that most fathers cherish. These are the events in a child's life most baseball scouts miss. He's gone—watching someone else's kids play baseball. The scout's wife who can do the job of both parents without complaint is the antithesis of the stereotype of the shallow ballplayer's wife: the teased-hair bimbo decorated with gobs of makeup and $6,000 breasts, carrying a Luis Vuitton bag and an attitude that screams "I'm Mrs. Ballplayer and You're Not!"

The Bodets reared three children by making the most of the time they had together, and this could have been one of those days together but for a dreaming father with a pal in a very high place.

For this particular assignment, the quality of the ballfield wasn't the source of Gib's question: "Why me?" Rather, it was the quality of the so-called prospect he was assigned to evaluate on that sunny Southern California day in late June of 1988.

Destination: Dodger Stadium.

Assignment: Evaluate the son of one of Tommy Lasorda's oldest and best friends.

Bodet had been down this road before. Several former big leaguers who ought to know better had asked him through the years to give his professional opinion on the merits of their sons' playing abilities. They seldom took it well when he broke the truth to them. They turned on him when he informed them that their sons were not prospects.

This task was particularly sticky. You see, Gib Bodet liked Tommy Lasorda. And not a little. He saw past the bluster of the loud lefty forever proclaiming, "Cut my veins open, and you'll see I bleed Dodger blue." Bodet saw something else when he peered beneath the loud layers of the face of the Dodgers and into the soul of that face. He saw a cowhide sphere with red stitches.

"Tommy's all baseball," Gib said of Lasorda. "And he's the most street-smart man I've ever known."

Lasorda isn't for everybody. Ben Wade, scouting director of the Dodgers throughout the '70s and '80s, didn't care for Lasorda any more than Lasorda cared for him. Maybe even a good deal less. Wade had given Gib the unenviable chore the previous night over the phone and told him he would be there himself to watch the "prospect" from suburban Philadelphia work out at Dodger Stadium.

It routinely has been reported that the Dodgers drafted Mike Piazza in the 62nd round as a favor to Lasorda. Wade was not of a mind to do Lasorda any favors. He drafted Piazza merely to get Lasorda off his back. He didn't want to have to deal with Lasorda's wrath each time he poked his head in the draft room and was asked, "Did you take Vince's boy yet?"

Vince was Vince Piazza; his boy was Michael. Lasorda tapped his connections to get Mike a spot on the prestigious University of Miami baseball team for a year. But even Ron Fraser, the Hurricanes' coach and a Lasorda pal, couldn't justify giving the kid playing time. He rotted on the bench. Mike then transferred to a junior college in Florida for a year. Getting drafted would enhance Mike's chances of drawing interest from another four-year college. Lasorda had scouts from the Dodgers and five other organizations evaluate Vince Piazza's son Michael, whose brother, Tommy, was Lasorda's godson. They all told Lasorda the same thing: "Tommy, the kid can't do anything." Nevertheless, Lasorda was able to nag Wade into using a draft choice on him, and since the kid was drafted, Wade had one of his top scouts check him out.

Bodet approached the assignment the way he had every other during a scouting career that began in the Tigers' organization in 1969, which is to say with an open mind and open eyes. He wasn't privy to the family background, a factor in making Lasorda believe the kid had more potential than anyone else saw. Lasorda figured that if the boy inherited the father's relentless drive he would exceed all expectations.

Lasorda knew that Vince had turned himself into a multi-millionaire starting with no more seed money than his $350 muster-out pay after a two-year overseas hitch in the military, no more schooling than a tenth-grade education. The son of a Sicilian immigrant, Vince found a job at a tire mill on the graveyard shift in 140-degree heat, losing ten pounds a night, drinking water to get the weight back. From there, he went straight to a garage he rented, and he worked on the junkers he bought off car dealers. He'd spruce them into condition and sell them. Seven days a week, seven years in a row, 18 hours a day, and he vows he never once peeked at the clock.

"I remember when Vince had only two jalopies on his little used car lot, and I'd have to help him sell one of them just so we could afford to buy lunch," Lasorda likes to joke.

Trying to make it selling refurbished cars on a dusty

lot across the street from a big-time, cutthroat dealership was no joke, though. The head of the dealership across the street had a connection with the state police, and when he spotted a shopper on Vince's lot, he would note the license plate, get the phone number from the state police, and call the customer at home. Or, if he didn't feel like going to all that effort, he'd take a shortcut by dialing the number to Vince's dealership in hopes the customer would leave when Vince answered the phone. Vince vowed he would leave the guy in his rearview mirror, told him as much, and went about doing so with street smarts and hustle. To hire salesmen for his dealerships he shopped for shoes and offered jobs to those whose pitches impressed him. He multiplied the fortune he made with car dealerships by investing in shopping malls and became a real estate tycoon. Lasorda knew all this and couldn't ignore it when projecting success for Vince's second-to-the-oldest of five boys, Michael.

Lasorda also knew that Michael approached baseball the way Vince approached the business world, by out-working everyone else. He knew that during the dead of winter in suburban Philadelphia, Michael would warm baseballs in the oven, a dozen at a time, so as to soften the sting to the hands when taking his nightly batting practice. Lasorda was well aware that no less an authority on hitting than Ted Williams had told Michael at the age of 16 that if he kept working hard at it, he would one day hit .280 in the major leagues.

Bodet knew none of this background, and Lasorda didn't see the need to fill him in, other than generally telling the scout the kid had "great makeup." Lasorda was in atypical low-key mode that day. Lasorda had confidence in Piazza's ability to swing the bat and believed every bit as deeply in his friend Gib's aptitude at judging hitters, by far the most difficult of all baseball tools to scout. Through the years, Bodet had many a friendly disagreement with scouting peers about the value of judging a hitter. Most of them would go something like this:

Scout: "Why bother scouting the bat? You don't know how they're gonna hit when the pitching gets better anyway. You're just guessing."

Gib: "You're selling yourself short if you don't project a kid's bat."

The great Branch Rickey, the patron saint of Dodger executives, of all baseball executives for that matter, would beg to differ with Mr. Bodet. Rickey, who authorized the signing of Jackie Robinson and broke baseball's color line in doing so, had definite beliefs regarding forecasting hitters that he passed on to Al Campanis, Lasorda, and countless other disciples. His beliefs, in essence, were not to bother trying to project how a young player is going to hit when the game speeds up. He believed it was best to sign players who could run and throw and as those players developed, the ones who continued to hit well as they climbed the minor league ladder would be the ones who made it to the big leagues. In the end, the thinking went, the Dodgers would have a team stocked full of players who could do it all. Rickey adhered to the same philosophy when running the St. Louis Cardinals and Pittsburgh Pirates.

"Rickey didn't have as much money as the Yankees, so the way he competed was with numbers," said Bodet, an avid baseball historian. "He signed more players than anybody else, got them cheaply, and if you couldn't run and throw, he wouldn't sign you. The only exception was he would sign catchers who couldn't run."

Rickey also believed in culling as much off-the-field background information as possible about players, much of the info coming from the players themselves. Looking back fondly on his days as a Dodgers minor leaguer at spring training camp in Vero Beach, Lasorda recalled being grilled by Rickey.

"Every night you would look at your schedule for the next day, and if your name was on the board to meet with Mr. Rickey in the morning, it was like meeting with the pope," Lasorda said. " He would play catch with you, put you through tests, show you how to throw a curveball, how to throw to spots, and the whole time he'd be asking you questions, wanting to know all about what your father is like, all about your mother."

Rickey was getting a feel for a player's makeup. Bodet and all good scouts do the same when evaluating young players on fields throughout the world, conversing with the players' best friends and girlfriends, brothers and sisters, getting them to reveal valuable information without them even knowing they were either fueling or dousing the scout's interest in the player in question.

On this particular day, makeup wasn't the issue at stake. Lasorda had tried that pitch with scouting friends from five other organizations and with a number of

Dodgers scouts. None of them saw enough ability to care about the kid's makeup. And if Bodet didn't see ability in the young Piazza boy, he wouldn't have cared about his makeup either. He would have been just another nice kid who couldn't play.

When Wade, the scouting director, called Bodet to tell him to come to Dodger Stadium to evaluate the late pick and told him the player's name, it didn't ring a bell.

"What can the kid do?" Bodet asked.

"He can't do anything," Wade said.

"He can't do anything? Then why do you want me to see him play?"

"He's Tommy's nephew."

Bodet to self: Why me?

There was a time when Bodet's eye for talent and feel for how players blend into a team would have made him a prime candidate for a general manager's job in baseball. That time had long since passed. He had the intelligence required for the job; he lacked the tolerance for politics. He's incapable of the country club laugh most modern day general managers have mastered. He'd prefer to tell the truth, no matter how difficult it might be for some to hear, than spin it in such a way as to come close to lying without technically lying.

He made the time to scout this suspect prospect because he didn't have any choice. Upon arriving at the ballpark the first face he saw was a familiar one: two chins, one full smile. He wore number 2 on his back; the interests of number 1 forever in his sights: Tommy Lasorda, among the most colorful, loudest, energetic figures in the game's rich history. They chatted, and a few minutes later, the kid walked into the clubhouse dressed in a pair of Dodgers pants, a blue sweatshirt, and a Dodgers cap. Lasorda and Mike Piazza embraced and kissed and the old-school scout grew all the more uncomfortable at the impending unenviable task of breaking the news to his friend and co-worker.

Lasorda introduced Bodet to Piazza and let the kid know the scout had come to watch him take batting practice. It amounted to a last chance for the college bust. Even if he weren't wearing a sweatshirt on such a hot summer day he would have been feeling the heat.

"Let's go," Lasorda said and led the boy and the scout out onto the field.

Joe Ferguson, a coach and loyal Lasorda soldier, threw batting practice. Loaded with baseball smarts, opinionated, sure of himself, and an imposing physical presence, Ferguson seemed to be made of major league managerial timber. His association with Lasorda, who would become a Hall of Fame manager, should have helped him to land a job in the big leagues. It never did. If anything, it worked against him, because Lasorda's combination of bluster and success inspired jealousy in so many corners. After Lasorda's retirement, Ferguson would spend much of his career managing in the minor leagues. On this day, his early afternoon job had him testing the young hitter with his best stuff. A former catcher, Ferguson remained in good enough shape to give the scout a decent read on a hitter taking BP hacks off of him.

"The first ball he hit I can still remember like he hit it yesterday," Bodet would say 15 years later. "He hit it off the left-center field fence at the 370 mark, hit it like a rocket. I don't know what the speed of the ball coming off that bat was, but I do know I had never seen a kid hit the ball that hard. The next ball he swung at crashed into the left-center field stands, about five rows deep. Then he popped up a pitch. Then he hit one into the blue seats in the back of the pavilion. Then he hit another ball into the blue seats."

And Bodet's mind began racing at the same warp speed as Piazza's bat was whirring through the strike zone. When, Bodet had asked himself, had he ever seen a young player hit a ball there? Never. He asked himself another question: When was the last time he saw a big league player who regularly hit a ball into the blue seats? Mickey Mantle, a quarter century earlier during the World Series.

"And these were not high flyballs the kid was hitting," remembers Bodet, who observed the workout from behind the hitting cage, near Lasorda. "The line drives just kept cooking."

Bobby Darwin, a former major leaguer blessed with good power, also took in the workout from a seat in the stands behind third base. Ben Wade, the scouting director, stood down the left field line, wearing a straw hat favored by baseball scouts as a means of protection against skin cancer.

"It was the most impressive batting practice I've ever seen a kid take," Bodet said in an interview during the 2003

Rich Pilling/Major League Baseball/Getty Images

MIKE PIAZZA

season. "And I've seen kids take pretty impressive batting practice. Ryan Klesko took batting practice at Dodger Stadium after the Braves drafted him. Very impressive. And he looked like a Little Leaguer compared to the one Piazza took."

After Piazza finished denting the outfield seats, he picked up a first baseman's glove and took grounders.

"He was okay," Bodet remembered. "He wasn't going to make anyone forget Gil Hodges, but his hands were okay."

Lasorda, wanting to give his friend's son every chance to make it, mentioned that the boy also had experience catching. Piazza donned the tools of ignorance and made throws to second base for the scouts while a kid stood at the plate batting left-handed. Bodet noted he stood up too erectly to throw and had an average arm, observations he deemed not too important because he had become so enamored of the late-round-steal-of-a-draft-choice's bat.

Bodet wasn't the only who saw the magic in Piazza's bat. The kid had been taking batting practice with the Dodgers for a few days, and Lasorda, encouraged by his equally impressed coaches, wanted to get him signed. He went over the head of Wade, the skeptical scouting director, and lobbied Peter O'Malley, the Dodgers' owner.

"Peter told Tommy he would have to go through the scouting department," Bodet said. "We couldn't go to Peter and suggest who should lead off, and Tommy couldn't go to Peter and tell him who we should sign. Tommy accepted that."

In Bodet, Lasorda knew he had a pair of eyes that would give an honest assessment of the young player both to him and to Wade. In Bodet, Lasorda also knew he had an apolitical man who wouldn't be afraid to disagree with Wade.

After Piazza dazzled with the workout, Lasorda and Bodet talked, and Lasorda liked what he heard from the scout.

"I'm going to go upstairs and tell Ben to sign this kid," Bodet said.

"Great," Lasorda said. "How much money?"

"I'm going to tell him $25,000," Bodet said of a figure that was unheard for a 62nd-round draft choice. "I'd take a $25,000 gamble on that bat."

Convincing Wade of that wasn't going to be easy. Convincing Wade that Piazza was anything more than a family favor was a challenge, especially considering that the heat had forced Wade upstairs into his air-conditioned office before the workout had ended. Bodet went to Wade's office ahead of Lasorda. Darwin joined Bodet in the elevator. It was the first chance for the scouts to discuss Piazza.

"What do you think of this guy's power?" Bodet asked Darwin.

"Jesus, Gib, he hit 'em where I didn't hit 'em," said Darwin, who hit 83 home runs in his big league career. "This kid's got some kind of juice."

The two men found Wade wiping sweat off his forehead.

"What do you think, Gib?" Wade asked.

"I don't think there's anything to think about, Ben," Bodet said. "Let's give the kid the money."

Shocked, Wade said with a pained expression, "The money? What are you talking about? We drafted this kid in the 62nd round."

"I don't care where we drafted him," Bodet said. "We don't have anybody who can swing the bat like this kid."

"That was just batting practice," Wade said, standing his ground.

"I don't care where we drafted the kid," Bodet persisted. "We got criticized for not drafting Eric Davis. Eric Davis looks like he's swinging a straw compared to this kid."

Then Wade asked the question often asked by baseball people looking for a reason not to like a player: "Where would you play him?"

"I'd play him at first base," Bodet said.

"Damn it, Gib, what's the matter with you?" Wade whined. "What's wrong with you? You signed Karros. Eric's going to be the first baseman of the future. He's hitting .300."

Bodet knew what he had just witnessed and wasn't going to back up an inch.

"I don't care what he's hitting and where he's hitting it," Bodet said. "The ball does not come off the bat like it comes off this kid's bat."

Wade asked Bodet how much money he would give him, which amounted to progress since the scouting director didn't think Piazza should be offered a dime when the post-workout discussion began.

"I'd give him twenty-five," Bodet said, triggering an explosion.

"What the hell are you doing throwing Peter's money around like that?" Wade hollered. "Twenty-five thousand? I thought you could scout when you came over here. You continue to make remarks like that, and I ought to fire your ass."

Wade turned to Darwin for support.

"Christ almighty, he'd give him twenty-five," Wade said, pointing to Bodet. "What would you give him?"

If Darwin were a politician first, a scout second, he would have answered not a dime, siding with his boss. He trusted his eyes instead.

"I'd give him forty," Darwin said.

At this point, Lasorda, who had heard some of Wade's hollering, entered the room to lobby for the young hitter.

"Are you going to sign him, Ben?" Lasorda asked.

"I've got to see him in a game," Wade answered.

"What the hell for, Ben?" Lasorda asked, his voice rising by the syllable. "He's been here all week. You saw what he did today and Gib's supposed to be one of your better scouts. He likes him. Now you're telling me you have to see him play in a game in Pennsylvania?"

Wade was convinced to sign Piazza and gave Dick Teed, a Connecticut-based scout, the assignment to sign him. A contract signing is a proud moment for a baseball prospect. The scout comes to the house, poses for pictures with the family, and joins a party. Teed's schedule was too filled with signings of players drafted much higher than Piazza. The best he could do was agree to meet the boy and his father at the airport, where Piazza signed his contract for $25,000.

This would not be the final slight of Piazza by the Dodgers. Once, during Instructional League, Piazza asked a hitting instructor if he could join a small group for a drill they were doing. "No," Piazza was told. "This is only for the top prospects." He never forgot that and used it as motivation. His playing time was sparse during his early minor league seasons, and he once bolted the team, inspiring a tongue-lashing from Lasorda. Minor league director Charlie Blaney was in favor of releasing Piazza at one point.

The case of Piazza illustrates the inexact nature of the science of forecasting baseball performance. His statistical performance as a college player and a young minor leaguer did not portend major league success. And had to be seen by several scouts before finally getting favorable reviews from Bodet and Darwin. If Bodet, the more influential of the two, had turned in a bad report on Piazza, no telling if Piazza ever would have been given a shot at a professional baseball career. He got his shot.

His signing was not newsworthy, considering all that was going on during that compelling summer of '88 for the World Champion Dodgers. Yet, the only player who would go on to have a Hall of Fame career who took batting practice for the Dodgers that year was the player chosen in the 62nd round because of his family connection to Lasorda.

The quick thinking by Lasorda, who insisted the kid

could become a catcher, played a part in Wade signing him. After all, first basemen with powerful bats were not hard to find. Catchers with numbers on the back of a baseball card to match those of Piazza are impossible to find.

His catching skills, never even average by major league standards, eroded to the point that the Mets felt they needed to pave the way for a position switch for Piazza and began to talk about how to implement the transition during the 2003 season. Proving he was no fit for New York, then Mets manager Art Howe told the press he planned to have Piazza start taking grounders at first base before he told the player. Big mistake. This triggered much discussion as to just what sort of first baseman Piazza would make. On my radio show I argued that the switch would be no big deal; Wally Matthews, my partner on the radio at the time, strongly disagreed. Wish I could have that one back.

Early in the 2004 season, when Piazza began splitting time between catcher and first base as he closed in on the record for home runs as a catcher, he handled his new position no better than Howe handled breaking the news. To put it kindly, Piazza was a butcher. He played the position as if cursed with two left feet. The footwork that kept him from taking advantage of a fairly strong arm as a catcher was even more noticeably bad when he tried to return to first base, the position of his youth. The experiment didn't last the season, and by 2005 Piazza was back to catching full-time for the Mets. By then, more than his defensive skills were fading.

On August 3, Piazza arrives at Shea Stadium for a game against the Brewers and for the first time since April of his rookie season in 1993, sees his name in the number 7 hole of a lineup card. Coincidentally, this was the night I picked to talk to him about playing first base, not one of his fondest baseball memories. No matter. The mellow Piazza is accommodating, insightful, and fully engaged in the conversation, as I've always found him to be.

I thought I'd start him off with a meatball.

I lob: "Playing first base a lot tougher than it looks?"

"Oh yeah," he returns the serve. "No question. I think it's a very underrated position as far as difficulty and responsibility. It's kind of like the umpire in a way. If you do a good job, nobody notices you. If you screw it up, everybody notices you."

Piazza, a lightning rod since the day he set foot in New York, made a lifeless franchise interesting, put bodies into seats that were empty, inspired countless back-page headlines, and was noticed a lot at first base. Oh, was he ever. And, as he says, notoriety is not a good thing for a first baseman.

He doesn't hesitate when asked why the position is harder than it looks.

"For me, the mobility was the biggest problem," he says. "I mean, my situation was different. I was a catcher who was non-mobile for 12 years, and then you go to first base in this league and you've got Juan Pierre bunting and Rafael Furcal and Luis Castillo and guys in that realm bunting, and not just bunting, but base-running in general. Having to move around and be mobile and make cutoffs and things like that."

Piazza had it all working against him. The creaky knees. The rusty glove. The stature that left him swimming in baseball's giant fishbowl as he clumsily tried to master a position he hadn't played in years and master it with fast men burning down the line and throws with such juice zipping toward him and batted balls whistling by him. And he did all this at a stage in his career when it was impossible to muster the sort of youthful hunger to get better that drove him as a young animal wounded by the "non-prospect" label pinned on him by Lasorda-bashers and uncreative thinkers who couldn't see past his position in the draft.

"I was a good first baseman when I was 20, 21," Piazza says. "No question I was better then. The mobility factor is a tough thing to overcome, especially after catching 1,500 games. I don't know too many guys who've made that switch smoothly after catching 1,500 games."

It's not that he didn't work at getting better. It's just that he wondered how far beyond repair he was as a first baseman, given the wear on his body. He worked at it enough to form opinions on what does and does not work.

"If I had the time and I took a lot of extra BP off the bat, maybe I could get better," he says, "because fungoes don't really do it. Fungoes are hit with backspin and game balls are hit with topspin. When you take fungoes, it's just half the story. It's more or less just getting your form down. True practice is catching balls off the bat."

Having played the position, and not well, in a fishbowl under hot lights, Piazza knows as well as anyone that first base is not a resting place for broken-down ballplayers who can't play anywhere else.

"I have a lot of respect for those guys," he says. "I always have. Look at Eric Karros in LA when I played with him. He was very underrated defensively and did a great job. He made great plays, and I thought did a great job. Now, after playing first base in this league, I've got even more respect for him. And it's tougher for a right-handed guy to play. That's why a guy like Derrek Lee, he's sort of taken for granted. I mean, he's an amazing athlete, and he's a great first baseman."

And those who are not so great will not get anything but empathy from Piazza, a designated hitter in training.

"We just saw the other day Jose Reyes throw the ball right past Chris Woodward," Piazza says. "Jose Reyes throws the ball over 80-something miles an hour. You could miss it. First base is a concentration position, and you can't take it lightly. You have to pay attention. In a matter of a split second, you have to be ready for anything from either a pickoff throw from the pitcher, who's really close to you, and the ball really gets to you in a hurry, to a ball off the bat of a left-handed pull hitter. I've had balls explode right by me and literally I put my glove up when it was three feet past me. In the big leagues, when you're playing in to hold the runner on, and a guy hits one down the line, that's not easy."

Piazza made playing first base look difficult, though he says with experience he found himself improving.

"I will say the only way I started getting a little better was when I went from a defensive mode to an offensive mode," he says. "I think you have to be aggressive and sort of attack the ball. You have to be the hunter, not the prey."

Everyone else remembers the bad plays of Piazza's brief eternity as a first baseman, and he packed a number of them into a short tenure. But he remembers the good feelings, too.

"When you make a great play, or you make a great stretch, or you scoop the ball, or you go up high, get the ball, and come down and tag the guy out, the infielders appreciate it," he says. "Acknowledgements from your peers and your teammates, those things for me are the most important. The fans are great when they give you an ovation, when they see you make a play, but when you have a guy go in the hole and fire a one-hopper, and you make a great play and he says, "Wow, that was a great play. Thanks a lot." That to me is one of the more satisfying things with the position."

Piazza's clumsy footwork impaired him at both positions, but he doesn't hesitate when asked which position requires better feet.

"First base," he says, "because of the fact that you have to be mobile. Footwork's important behind the plate too, but if you have a decent arm you can get away with some things. It hurts when you're taller in stature, catcher-wise. I'm bigger framed than most of the guys. Very few guys that I can recall in my career were big catchers who were agile. I think the cutoff point is somewhere around six feet tall. I'm 6'2". A catcher gets over six feet tall, and he gets sort of top heavy. It's not impossible, but it is tough. When you get taller you have to be more athletic, and I'm definitely not the most versatile athlete. I admire guys when I see like defensive backs, the athletic prowess that they have is something I admire. I'm somewhat of an athlete, but I'm not a true athlete, so I can admire that."

He's an athlete, however, with a bat in his hands. A proud athlete, despite the shrinking numbers. On this night in August, his demotion to seventh in the order is an acknowledgement he is not the RBI bat he once was. Yet, he's still Mike Piazza. Tell him he can't do something, then sit back and watch him do it. Draft him in the 62nd round, forbid him from partaking in special batting instruction with the "prospects," and then watch him leave all those higher draft choices in his wake. Tell him he can't possibly catch in the big leagues, and then watch him become a perennial All-Star catcher. Bat him seventh for the first time in 12 years and watch him crush a pitch deep into the picnic area, driven there as much by pride as by muscle on a night the Mets would fall short by a run, through no fault of Piazza.

To know Piazza's history is to expect a tape-measure home run from the number 7 hole on this potentially embarrassing evening. Put a hurdle in his way, and then watch him stride over it. Except for one: He couldn't clear the hurdle known as first base. He failed.

"In theory, on paper, it's probably pretty easy to imagine, but in reality, it's not an easy switch," he says.

Maybe, I wondered, he had some unfinished business

he planned on getting around to polishing off. Maybe he would give the position one more try.

"Oh, I don't know, I don't know," he says, meaning he knows, he knows, and the answer is no, no, not now, not in a million years, not ever again. "I will say this: It is tough to teach an old dog new tricks."

7TH

The Water Cooler of Baseball

Football players get to talk to each other whether their unit is on the field or off it. After each play, they convene in the huddle as they catch their breaths and listen to or give assignments for the next play. The conversations are all business. Basketball players are in constant communication with each other as plays unfold. They act as each other's eyes to promote teamwork defensively and bark out and listen to plays called offensively. Again, all business.

How much a baseball player talks and what he talks about while on the field depends on what position he plays. The catcher talks to his pitcher with his fingers. He flashes a series of signs that tell the pitcher which pitch to throw and where its vertical and horizontal location should be. The pitcher talks back to the catcher with his head, nodding agreement or disagreement with the pitch selection. If that doesn't work, they call time, meet at the edge of the mound and get their signals straight. They also can hold conversations on the mound to buy time for the relief pitcher who hasn't thrown enough pitches in the bullpen to get loose enough to enter the game.

The middle infielders will talk to each other either

with body language or quick words to determine who covers second when a runner is on first. They will sometimes even greet a baserunner with a quick hello. The third baseman doesn't have much to say and seldom has anybody to whom to talk when manning his position. Outfielders stand so far away from any other players the only words they say on the field are, "Got it!" when chasing down a flyball.

The baseball player who wants to socialize and converse about a wide array of topics that include (but are not even close to being limited to) baseball needs to buy himself a first baseman's glove.

First base is the water cooler of baseball. It's where most of the game's most trivial and most poignant conversations take place, provided you don't mind constant interruptions by the responsibilities created by the ongoing game. First base is to baseball what Cheers was to television—a great place to hold conversations, between sips at Cheers and between pitches at first base. It's the most social of all baseball positions. The first baseman is baseball's unofficial greeter, psychologist, and sometimes even hitting instructor to slumping ballplayers.

"The one thing about playing first base that I really like is you meet different types of people," says Jim Thome of the Chicago White Sox. "The funny ones, the serious ones, the outgoing ones, the quiet ones. For me, the fun part about it is meeting those different types of players and seeing what they're really like. You can't do that playing any other position."

Enemies become friends between pitches and turn back into enemies from the time the pitcher gets rid of the ball to the time he gets it back. What in the world are the fielder and the baserunner talking about down there anyway? Anything and everything. Small talk. Funny talk. Serious talk. Baseball pointers. And occasionally, gamesmanship takes place, wherein the fielder attempts to engage the runner in conversation to distract him in order to pick him off base. According to major leaguers past and present, such gamesmanship rarely happens and far more rarely works.

"Stargell," onetime basestealer Davey Lopes said of ex-Pirates slugger and Hall of Famer Willie Stargell from his seat in the visiting dugout in Philadelphia. Lopes at once was on the verge of a roll of the eyes and a laugh. "He would always try to get me to look for the Goodyear blimp to distract me into getting picked off. 'Hey, Davey, here comes the blimp,' he would say. I would say, 'All right, Willie, I've talked to you enough. I'm going on the next pitch. See ya.' And then I'd go on the next pitch."

Said Rockies first baseman Todd Helton: "It has happened that way inadvertently. You'll be talking to a guy about something, the pitcher happens to throw over, and you get him out. I don't purposely try to do that. If that works, the guy probably shouldn't be at this level."

Luis Sojo, who coached third base for the Yankees during the '05 season, spent much of his career in the middle of the infield and has been a first baseman during the winter in recent years in his native Venezuela.

"You try some different ways to get their concentration

off," Sojo said. "Sometimes, you know they're going to take off if it's a fast runner, to be able to say something to him to distract him, it's part of the first baseman's

MICKEY HATCHER

job. If you're a runner, you're going to say something to the first baseman. If you're a first baseman, you're going to say something to the runner. It doesn't matter, he's still going to go. It doesn't work, but you try it anyway."

Mickey Hatcher, a utility man who played first base for the World Champion Los Angeles Dodgers in the 1988 World Series, said he didn't make a habit of trying to fool the runner because he figured it wouldn't work.

"I did see it work once, though," Hatcher said. "Jose Canseco was the runner."

Imagine that.

Hatcher was a chatterbox at first base. If he wasn't talking in an attempt to steal an out, what was he talking about? Asked to give an example of what he might have said to a runner, Hatcher responded: "How about that chick up there in the third row."

Then he flashed the smile that was just one of the many reasons Dodgers fans found him so endearing.

"You know, baseball talk!" he said.

The runner can be a sounding board for the fielder

129

and vice versa.

"I remember times I'm over there, the sun's setting over the third base side and the pitcher's on the mound, you say to the runner, 'Man, I hope he doesn't throw a ball over here right now.' I was always chirping over there," Hatcher said.

Helton isn't as chatty.

"It's all about a person's personality," Helton said. "It may sound weird, but I'm kind of shy in the fact that if I don't know somebody, I guess I don't like small talk. If I don't small talk, I just say hello."

TODD HELTON

Helton is, however, a good listener, especially if the person doing the talking has credibility on the topic of conversation.

"This year I've struggled more at the plate than I've ever struggled, and I've gotten a lot of tips over there, from first base coaches to guys on first," he said. "They volunteer them. I would never solicit them from an opposing player. They're just trying to be nice. I was really struggling, and I think they were doing it because they felt sorry for me, which is pretty sad. I got a tip from one other really good first baseman the other day and I started laughing. He asked what I was laughing about, and I said it's just kind of funny that an opposing player is trying to get me out of my slump. I was laughing because it had come to that. I'd fallen that far down."

The opposing player lending a hand to help pick him up: Albert Pujols.

"He definitely knows his hitting," Helton said.

When Helton reaches first base, he talks with one of the game's friendlier men, Rockies first base coach Dave Collins.

"The conversations that go on at first base are interesting, just from the standpoint they can be about what he's going through individually or what somebody else is going through," Collins said. "His team, his teammate, an issue with a teammate, an issue with the manager, or it can be something that you're joking about. You can be joking about different things. I know Sean Casey well, and a lot of times we're joking around about something that's happening in a game. It's the people you remember in the game and the character they have, not so much the numbers they put up."

Collins consistently ranked among league leaders in stolen bases during his playing career.

The base stealers are the ones who never talk to the first baseman," Collins said. "The non-base stealers are the ones who'll talk all the time. The good base runners will never talk to the first baseman. The below-average runners will talk to the first baseman because they don't have pride in their base running. When I got on first base, speed was a big part of my game. I had to steal bases. My whole focus was I dare you to throw me out even if you pitch out. It's a mindset that has nothing to do with speed in the legs. It has to do with speed in the mind and speed in the heart. You've got to be daring. You've got to be willing to take on the catcher and the pitcher and get to second base when they know you're going to run. When you get thrown out, you've got to be able to come back and say hey I'll do it again."

Asked if all-time stolen base king Rickey Henderson was a big talker at first base, Collins replied, "He wasn't there long enough to talk."

Collins has engaged many an opposing first baseman in conversation.

"It doesn't always have to be about baseball," Collins said. "It can be something that's personal that you're willing to share with somebody that you know and you trust and you're able to talk to them. And the thing that's great, you can turn your attention around a second later and focus on what you're doing in the game. And after the pitch, you're right back into your conversation. Boom, you go back into that again."

Collins ranks Thome among his favorite conversation partners at first base.

"I love talking to Jim Thome," Collins said. "The thing that separates Jim Thome from a lot of guys is if he strikes out he still comes out and talks to you, and he doesn't let one at-bat affect his personality. He'll talk about anything and everything."

Collins said the most memorable talk he had with Thome at first base had nothing to do with baseball. It was far more personal than any baseball conversation ever could be.

"I hadn't seen him in a year," Collins remembered. "The first thing he brought up to me was the fact that his mom had passed away. He talked about what his mother meant to him and how tough it was to deal with what he'd been going through. He talked about how his mother would always talk about the golden rule, treat others the way you like to be treated. I told him: 'You know what, she did a great job because you're as good a guy as there is in the game. You can be proud she was your mom because she did a great job.' We talked about his mom for a couple of innings."

Most conversations at first base aren't nearly as personal and many revolve around the greatest of all baseball mysteries, even to those who do it the best, the mystery of hitting a baseball. It didn't take Don Mattingly long to spit out a name when he was asked what base runner from his era did the most talking.

"Brett Butler was always talking," Mattingly said. "He was always whining about hitting the ball hard every day and not getting any hits. Stuff like—18 of the last 25 balls I've hit have been right on the nose, and I only got three hits to show for it."

The chattiest first baseman in the game today?

"Sean Casey, no doubt," Gary Sheffield said from his Yankee Stadium locker.

Helton: "Casey's the league leader."

Ken Griffey Jr.: "Ask anybody and they'll tell you Sean Casey. You ask everybody in baseball and you'll get the same answer—Sean Casey."

As mentioned in chapter four, Griffey asked four different teammates who passed by him in the hall and all four answered Casey in such a way as to suggest the answer was so obvious there was no point in asking the question.

Seven years before the 2005 steroid hearings before Congress stripped the innocence from the summer of 1998, a baseball season during which Mark McGwire and

SEAN CASEY

Sammy Sosa captivated a nation by shattering Roger Maris's long-standing single-season home run record and dueling for supremacy, Casey had a conversation he still relishes.

"One of the coolest memories I have at first base is from my rookie year," Casey said. "I had gotten hit in the eye and went down to the minors. When I came back up from the minors, the Cardinals came to town. I was so excited that Mark McGwire walked because that meant I was going to get to talk to him. [Reds' manager] Jack McKeon's yelling, 'Hey, hey, play behind him,' and I don't even hear him. I went over to first and said, 'Hey, Mac, how you doing?' And he says, 'Hey, Sean.' I was like, 'Yeah, he knows my name!' I said: 'Hey, this has been a great season. It's been so fun watching.' So we're talking and I thought, This is great, Mark McGwire, bigger than life, and he's talking to me. My rookie year. I'm talking to Mark McGwire, and he's talking back to me. I was in awe. McKeon couldn't get my attention. Then the bench coach is yelling. He couldn't get my attention. Finally, the whole team's yelling at me. I was so enthralled in the conversation I'm not hearing any of it. Finally, McGwire taps me and says, 'Hey, uh, I think they want you to play behind me.' I was like, 'Oh, okay, I'm sorry.' Jack's screaming, 'What the hell! We've been yelling at you for five minutes. Get in the game!'"

It's always bittersweet for Casey when Lance Berkman of the Houston Astros reaches first base. On the one hand, Casey wants his pitcher to get him out, but if somebody has to get on base, Casey figures, it might as well be someone whose company he enjoys.

"We have some great conversations about his wife and his girls," Casey said. "He's a great dude. He's usually not stealing a base, so we get a chance to talk. He's playing first now, so we get a chance to talk even more."

Casey seizes every opportunity he can to expand his knowledge on baseball's most mysterious art.

"I'm always picking guys brains about hitting," Casey said. "I was talking to Alex Rodriguez during a spring training game, and he was talking about Edgar Martinez driving the ball up the middle. I was talking to Tony Gwynn about hitting. I remember him coming to first base when he was scuffling, and he was hitting .330. Think about that. He's hitting .330 and for him that meant he was scuffling. He said, 'I don't know what's wrong with me.'

He hit two home runs against us that day, then he got another hit, and when he got to first he said, 'Dude, you know I'm scuffling when I hit two home runs.' I was like: 'Dude, I wish I was scuffling like that.' He was amazing."

Casey has found the cure to slumps by conversing with base runners.

"A few years ago in Colorado, I remember I was struggling and I asked Helton, 'What do you do when you're in a slump? Do you gear up or do you back it down?' He said, 'I just try to see it and hit the ball hard.' I remember simplifying things after that conversation. I was at the point where I was asking myself, where's my hands, where's my feet, and you can't do that. After talking to Helton, I had a huge series. Helton, the third day in, said, 'Don't ever talk to me again about hitting when you're playing us.' I'll never forget that."

Conversations between opponents at first base can be as trivial as where they ate dinner the night before or even where they like to eat dinner in the next town on one team or the other's schedule. The chats can be as personal and as friendly as inquiring how the player's children are doing on their Little League teams or as practical as talking about how they treat their mitts to make them game ready.

There is no official glove doctor on major league baseball teams. Sometimes it's the equipment manager. On many other clubs, the trainer is the most skilled at treating damaged gloves. No position, with the possible exception of a catcher, requires more glove maintenance than the first baseman. There also is no set length a player prefers to use his mitt before deciding to move onto a new one, though the most common length of time seems to be one season.

For the Rockies, trainer Keith Ducker is the glove doctor.

"I usually use one a year, but this year for some reason it got too soft," Todd Helton said. "A lot of guys like a soft first baseman's mitt. I like to have a backbone in it. I don't want it to pull back on me when I go to pick a ball. I have a bad hand, and every time I caught the ball it hurt real bad because it was too soft. I'm very, very particular with my glove."

Most of his peers are as well. They have different methods of breaking in their first baseman's mitts.

"I loosen up everything in the hand and play catch with it," Helton said. "Before the game I put a little dab of petroleum jelly on the inside of the pocket, to give a little stick to it. I need all the help I can get."

Casey gets attached to his mitt, so it takes more than one season of use to convince him he needs to move onto a newer model.

"I've had this one for three years," he said. "The Rawlings model that I use breaks in pretty easily, but I don't like to switch. Once you get comfortable, you can't really let it go. When it starts to break down and gets unrepairable, that's when I go to another one."

Casey said he has "two go-to guys" that he turns to when he needs to see a mitt doctor. Starting pitcher Aaron Harang is one and bullpen catcher Mike Sefansky is the other.

Rich Pilling/Major League Baseball/Getty Images

JIM THOME

"Aaron is a big-time glove repair man," Casey said. "He loves it. And Mike Stefansky's awesome too."

Casey doesn't play catch with his mitt to break it in, as so many of his peers do. He wants the baseball cooking a little hotter than it does in a simple catch, so he gives it to Stefansky and has him catch bullpens with it.

"I tell Mike Stefansky I want a deep pocket, and he tells me when it's ready," Casey said. "When he thinks it's good enough, he gives it back to me."

Jim Thome simply plays catch with his glove and when it feels broken in to him he brings it into the game.

"I baby it, caress it, that's how you've got to treat your glove," Thome said. "I just put a little bit of the glove oil on it to make sure it's smooth and moist. I'll do that maybe once a week and it's big-time important to do that. Usually, I go through a glove a year. Toward the end of the year, the strings will come loose and when that happens, the strings need to be replaced by the trainers."

How to treat a glove, what method to use to "baby it, caress it" can be among the conversations discussed at first base. Those conversations, and just about any other topics that pop into the heads of the fielders and the base runners, are what take place between pitches at first base, the friendliest, most social position in the game of baseball.

8TH

Three Great Ones:
Foxx, Gehrig, and Greenberg

First, Hurricane Frances dumped its fury on Vero Beach, tearing the roof off the charming home of Elden and Mildred Auker and blowing away much of the memorabilia collection of a man who collected only pictures and keepsakes from the friends with whom he played baseball in the 1930s and early '40s for the Detroit Tigers, Boston Red Sox, and St. Louis Browns. Three weeks later, days after Elden's 94th birthday, Hurricane Jeanne damaged the new home the Aukers were to move into at the turn of the year. And so Elden and Mildred Auker, voted Joe College and Betty Co-Ed from Kansas State University's Class of 1932, became vagabonds, moving from one temporary residence to the next, until the home of Mildred's nephew and niece, Mr. and Mrs. George Purcell, was ready for them to move into. In the days after one of the hurricanes, the Aukers and their relatives were forced to take shelter in a warehouse, where rats crawled on the concrete floor. Finally, a year after Hurricane Frances' rude visit to Vero Beach, the Aukers were able to move into their new home.

The hurricanes did nothing to dull Auker's razor-sharp mind. He turned 95 on Sept. 21, 2005, and the way

Transcendental Graphics

JIMMIE FOXX

he talked about the great first basemen of his era, it was clear those bygone days seemed as if they had occurred just last week.

Auker, the last living member of the World Champion 1935 Tigers, first was asked to describe the body types of Lou Gehrig, Jimmie Foxx, and Hank Greenberg, three of the greatest first basemen to play in any era. Gehrig, of course, starred on the great Yankee teams of the '20s and '30s, and his name is still well known even to casual fans of the game. Jimmie Foxx, during that time, was considered just as good as Gehrig, belting home runs for the Philadelphia Athletics and the Boston Red Sox. Greenberg was slightly less well known, because he played in Detroit rather than in an Eastern media center. The question about the body types led Auker to discuss the differences in their swings.

"Gehrig had big calves, big lower legs, a very small waist, and a powerful chest," Auker started. "Jimmie Foxx had terrific arms, and legs like a beast. We called him The Beast. Jimmie'd take his arm and curl it up to make a muscle the size of a cannon ball. Hank was a tall, slender guy with flat feet. He stood flat-footed, and he had a long swing, much different from the others. Gehrig really set his feet down into the ground. Hank stood flat-footed, and Jimmie stood normal and had great wrists, terrific wrists. Hank did not have powerful legs and was not exceptionally powerful with his arms. He was big and strong and he had a great, big swing. When Hank got ahold of it he could really rip it. His power came from his long swing."

Transcendental Graphics

LOU GEHRIG

Gehrig and Foxx didn't need long swings to generate tremendous power.

"Lou had great arms, a real muscleman," Auker said. "So was Foxxie. They weren't tall like Hank. But they both had such great wrists they could almost hit the ball out of the catcher's mitt. Hank's height helped him to become such a good first baseman. He wasn't a natural. He was a little clumsy at first, but he worked so hard at it he became a very good first baseman. And he never really got the credit he deserved for his fielding ability. He was such a big target over there the shortstop, second baseman, or third baseman could throw it anywhere in the area and Hank could pick it up. Gehrig was a good fielder, and he was a real hustler. Foxx could play any position. He was a catcher also, and he even had a little experience pitching. He was just a great all-around athlete. He came up when he was 18 years old."

Comparing the three as base runners, Auker said, "Foxx was such a great all-around athlete, I guess I'd have to say probably Foxx was the best. Lou was a good base runner. He was built close to the ground and had powerful legs. And he was such a hustler. Hank wasn't fast. He was too big, and his feet were as flat as a pancake. If we had a doubleheader, he came out of the first game and would jump right up on the table to get his feet rubbed to get ready for the second game. Those big feet always gave him trouble."

Their body types contributed to different swings and abilities running the bases and their personality differences led to different amounts of interaction at baseball's most social position when a runner reached first base.

"Lou was quiet," Auker said. "He would talk, but he wouldn't start much of a conversation. He was quiet, but a wonderful guy. Jimmie was very gregarious. Everybody loved him and would always talk with him over there."

Auker, mindful that Gehrig was a low-ball hitter, threw at his feet to try to make him uncomfortable and tried to keep the ball low and away on most hitters. He pitched the baseball underhanded well enough to win 130 games in 10 seasons, but as well as he pitched a baseball, he continues to do an even better job of pitching baseball stories, not all of which have happy endings. It still pains Auker to reflect on the tough moments his friends, the first basemen, encountered. He pitches riveting stories about all three.

The year was 1939, Auker's only season with the Boston Red Sox. The Yankees were making their first trip of the season to Fenway Park.

"Lou was in the tunnel, smoking a cigarette, with his foot up on the step, about to run out onto the field, when I snuck up behind him," Auker recalled. "He was always sneaking up behind people and lifting them up, so I used to do the same to him. Well, this time, I snuck up behind him, gave him a bear hug, and he fell right to the ground, just collapsed. He said, 'Elden don't do that.' I helped him back onto his feet and asked him, 'Lou, what the hell's the matter with you?' He said, 'Oh, Elden, I don't know, but I know there's something wrong. I feel so weak. I couldn't hit a ball out of the infield all spring.

Transcendental Graphics

HANK GREENBERG

I don't know what it is, but I know something's just not right.' That was the last time I ever spoke to Lou. Shortly after that, the Yankees went to Detroit and Lou took a side trip to the Mayo Clinic in Minnesota. That's where he was diagnosed with the disease."

The Aukers named their only child James Emory Auker after James Emory Foxx, Elden's roommate with the Red Sox during the 1939 season.

"Jimmie Foxx was as nice a man as you would ever a want to meet," Auker said. "A real gentleman. He was the kind of guy who would do anything for you and not think twice about it. He didn't deserve the treatment he got from his wife that year. She never did come to Boston to see him, but he had a picture of her, and she was a stunning, stunning woman. And a real social climber. She was in love with a banker from Philadelphia, and she was trying to get out of her marriage to Jimmie. She would call in the middle of the night, haranguing him all the time in the middle of the night. To get him for every penny he had, she accused him of all sorts of things he never did. I knew he didn't do them because I roomed with him and knew where he was at all times. On top of all that, Jimmie had invested in a golf course with a partner and that turned out to be a real drain on him. They were always asking for more money. The only time you couldn't see what a tough year it was for him was when he had a bat in his hands. One night he was up in the middle of the night with a nosebleed, and I called the trainer to come up and take a look at it. The trainer came up and stuffed Jimmie's nose full of cotton to stop the bleeding. Jimmie was up most of the night, and I didn't expect him to come to the ballpark. Well, he came to the game all right. He wasn't on time to take batting practice, but he was on time to hit a line drive clear into the center field bleachers at Sportsman's Park in St. Louis his first time up. That ball went 450 feet if it went a foot. I came to find out he died choking on a ham sandwich without a penny to his name. They say he took to drinking. We went out once in a while for a beer or two, but I never saw him drink heavily at all. It was a shame. He was such a terrific guy. Never had an ill word to say about anybody. He deserved so much better than that."

Auker said Greenberg initially was clumsy at first base and had a particularly difficult time with popups. But thanks to a strong work ethic, he cured the problem and became good with the glove, thanks to daily 9 a.m. sessions with coach Del Baker, one of the Greenberg's minor league managers.

"Today you hear a lot about the prejudice Hank faced during his playing career because he was Jewish," Auker said. "Well, Hank kept that all to himself and never would say anything about it. He was a target of a lot of anti-Semitic sentiment, but he didn't say anything about it. I do remember one incident when the Chicago White Sox were in town. They were real bench jockeys, led by the biggest bench jockey of them all, their player/manager Jimmy Dykes. Well, Hank was running down to first base in front of the White Sox dugout, and one of them called him a 'big, yellow Jew bastard.' Hank came back to our dugout and didn't say a word about it. I was familiar with

Hank's post-game routine because my locker was right near his. He would come in after the game and have the trainer rub his feet. He was so flat-footed his feet were always killing him after the game. This time, he took his jersey off, left on his sweatshirt under it, and slipped into slippers and walked out the door of the clubhouse. I figured he had visitors waiting for him. After a while, he came back in the door and went about his normal routine. I didn't think another thing about it until the next day when one of the White Sox told me Hank went into their clubhouse on a mission to find out who said the derogatory remarks. I was told Hank went into their clubhouse and demanded the culprit stand up and confess his cowardly act. Everyone stayed seated, so Hank walked around the room and stared into the face of everyone on the team without saying a word. On his way out the door, he turned around, looked back at them sternly, then returned to our clubhouse. Hank never would have said a word to us about it. We only found out because the White Sox talked about it. That's how Hank was. He didn't want what he had to go through to hinder the team in any way."

Summing up his pals on first base in one word, Auker said: "Gentlemen."

Mildred Auker chose another word: "Handsome."

9TH

The Lists

A meeting of Hall of Fame first basemen: Lou Gehrig of the New York Yankees sweeps a tag on George Sisler of the St. Louis Browns during a game circa 1926.

Hall of Famers

Adrian Cap Anson

Bats: Right Throws: Right
Height: 6' 0" Weight: 227 lb.
Born: April 17, 1852 in Marshalltown, IA
Died: April 14, 1922 in Chicago, IL
Hall of Fame Inductee — 1939

Year	Ag	Tm	Lg	G	AB	R	H	2B	3B	HR	RBI	BA	OBP	SLG	TB
1871	19	ROK	NA	25	120	29	39	11	3	0	16	.325	.336	.467	56
1872	20	ATH	NA	46	217	60	90	10	7	0	50	.415	.455	.525	114
1873	21	ATH	NA	52	254	53	101	9	2	0	36	.398	.409	.449	114
1874	22	ATH	NA	55	259	51	87	8	3	0	37	.336	.346	.390	101
1875	23	ATH	NA	69	326	84	106	15	3	0	58	.325	.333	.390	127
1876	24	CHC	NL	66	309	63	110	9	7	2	59	.356	.380	.450	139
1877	25	CHC	NL	59	255	52	86	19	1	0	32	.337	.360	.420	107
1878	26	CHC	NL	60	261	55	89	12	2	0	40	.341	.372	.402	105
1879	27	CHC	NL	51	227	40	72	20	1	0	34	.317	.323	.414	94
1880	28	CHC	NL	86	356	54	120	24	1	1	74	.337	.362	.419	149
1881	29	CHC	NL	84	343	67	137	21	7	1	82	.399	.442	.510	175
1882	30	CHC	NL	82	348	69	126	29	8	1	83	.362	.397	.500	174
1883	31	CHC	NL	98	413	70	127	36	5	0	68	.308	.336	.419	173
1884	32	CHC	NL	112	475	108	159	30	3	21	102	.335	.373	.543	258
1885	33	CHC	NL	112	464	100	144	35	7	7	108	.310	.357	.461	214
1886	34	CHC	NL	125	504	117	187	35	11	10	147	.371	.433	.544	274
1887	35	CHC	NL	122	472	107	164	33	13	7	102	.347	.422	.517	244
1888	36	CHC	NL	134	515	101	177	20	12	12	84	.344	.400	.499	257
1889	37	CHC	NL	134	518	100	161	32	7	7	117	.311	.414	.440	228
1890	38	CHC	NL	139	504	95	157	14	5	7	107	.312	.443	.401	202
1891	39	CHC	NL	136	540	81	157	24	8	8	120	.291	.378	.409	221
1892	40	CHC	NL	146	559	62	152	25	9	1	74	.272	.354	.354	198
1893	41	CHC	NL	103	398	70	125	24	2	0	91	.314	.415	.384	153
1894	42	CHC	NL	83	340	82	132	28	4	5	99	.388	.457	.538	183
1895	43	CHC	NL	122	474	87	159	23	6	2	91	.335	.408	.422	200
1896	44	CHC	NL	108	402	72	133	18	2	2	90	.331	.407	.400	161
1897	45	CHC	NL	114	424	67	121	17	3	3	75	.285	.379	.361	153
Totals				2523	10277	1996	3418	581	142	97	2076	.333	.393	.445	4574

Transcendental Graphics

Jake Beckley

Bats: Left Throws: Left
Height: 5' 10" Weight: 200 lb.
Born: August 4, 1867 in Hannibal, MO
Died: June 25, 1918 in Kansas City, MO
Hall of Fame Inductee — 1971

Year	Ag	Tm	Lg	G	AB	R	H	2B	3B	HR	RBI	BA	OBP	SLG	TB
1888	20	PIT	NL	71	283	35	97	1	5	3	027	.343	.363	.417	118
1889	21	PIT	NL	123	522	91	157	24	10	9	97	.301	.345	.437	228
1890	22	PBB	PL	121	516	109	167	38	22	9	120	.324	.381	.535	276
1891	23	PIT	NL	133	554	94	162	20	19	4	73	.292	.353	.419	232
1892	24	PIT	NL	151	614	102	145	21	19	10	96	.236	.288	.381	234
1893	25	PIT	NL	131	542	108	164	32	19	5	106	.303	.386	.459	249
1894	26	PIT	NL	131	533	121	183	36	18	7	120	.343	.412	.518	276
1895	27	PIT	NL	129	530	104	174	31	19	5	110	.328	.381	.487	258
1896	28	PIT	NL	59	217	44	55	7	5	3	32	.253	.349	.373	81
		NYG	NL	46	182	37	55	8	4	5	38	.302	.352	.473	86
		TOT	NL	105	399	81	110	15	9	8	70	.276	.351	.419	167
1897	29	NYG	NL	17	68	8	17	2	3	1	11	.250	.301	.412	28
		CIN	NL	97	365	76	126	17	9	7	76	.345	.395	.499	182
		TOT	NL	114	433	84	143	19	12	8	87	.330	.380	.485	210
1898	30	CIN	NL	118	459	86	135	20	12	4	72	.294	.348	.416	191
1899	31	CIN	NL	134	513	87	171	27	16	3	99	.333	.393	.466	239
1900	32	CIN	NL	141	558	98	190	26	10	2	94	.341	.389	.434	242
1901	33	CIN	NL	140	580	78	178	36	13	3	79	.307	.346	.429	249
1902	34	CIN	NL	129	531	82	175	23	7	5	69	.330	.377	.427	227
1903	35	CIN	NL	120	459	85	150	29	10	2	81	.327	.384	.447	205
1904	36	STL	NL	142	551	72	179	22	9	1	67	.325	.375	.403	222
1905	37	STL	NL	134	514	48	147	20	10	1	57	.286	.333	.370	190
1906	38	STL	NL	87	320	29	79	16	6	0	44	.247	.283	.334	107
1907	39	STL	NL	32	115	6	24	3	0	0	7	.209	.222	.235	27
Totals				2386	9526	1600	2930	473	243	86	1575	.308	.361	.435	4147

Jim Bottomley

Bats: Left Throws: Left
Height: 6' 0" Weight: 180 lb.
Born: April 23, 1900 in Oglesby, IL
Died: December 11, 1959 in St.Louis, MO
Hall of Fame Inductee — 1974

Transcendental Graphics

Year	Ag	Tm	Lg	G	AB	R	H	2B	3B	HR	RBI	BA	OBP	SLG	TB
1922	22	STL	NL	37	151	29	49	8	5	5	35	.325	.358	.543	82
1923	23	STL	NL	134	523	79	194	34	14	8	94	.371	.425	.535	280
1924	24	STL	NL	137	528	87	167	31	12	14	111	.316	.362	.500	264
1925	25	STL	NL	153	619	92	227	44	12	21	128	.367	.413	.578	358
1926	26	STL	NL	154	603	98	180	40	14	19	120	.299	.364	.506	305
1927	27	STL	NL	152	574	95	174	31	15	19	124	.303	.387	.509	292
1928	28	STL	NL	149	576	123	187	42	20	31	136	.325	.402	.628	362
1929	29	STL	NL	146	560	108	176	31	12	29	137	.314	.391	.568	318
1930	30	STL	NL	131	487	92	148	33	7	15	97	.304	.368	.493	240
1931	31	STL	NL	108	382	73	133	34	5	9	75	.348	.403	.534	204
1932	32	STL	NL	91	311	45	92	16	3	11	48	.296	.350	.473	147
1933	33	CIN	NL	145	549	57	137	23	9	13	83	.250	.311	.395	217
1934	34	CIN	NL	142	556	72	158	31	11	11	78	.284	.324	.439	244
1935	35	CIN	NL	107	399	44	103	21	1	1	49	.258	.294	.323	129
1936	36	SLB	AL	140	544	72	162	39	11	12	95	.298	.354	.476	259
1937	37	SLB	AL	65	109	11	26	7	0	1	12	.239	.346	.330	36
Totals				**1991**	**7471**	**1177**	**2313**	**465**	**151**	**219**	**1422**	**.310**	**.369**	**.500**	**3737**

Dan Brouthers

Bats: Left Throws: Left
Height: 6' 2" Weight: 207 lb.
Born: May 8, 1858 in Sylvan Lake, NY
Died: August 2, 1932 in E.Orange, NJ
Hall of Fame Inductee — 1945

Transcendental Graphics

Year	Ag	Tm	Lg	G	AB	R	H	2B	3B	HR	RBI	BA	OBP	SLG	TB
1879	21	TRO	NL	39	168	17	46	12	1	4	17	.274	.278	.429	72
1880	22	TRO	NL	3	12	0	2	0	0	0	1	.167	.231	.167	2
1881	23	BUF	NL	65	270	60	86	18	9	8	45	.319	.361	.541	146
1882	24	BUF	NL	84	351	71	129	23	11	6	63	.368	.403	.547	192
1883	25	BUF	NL	98	425	85	159	41	17	3	97	.374	.397	.572	243
1884	26	BUF	NL	94	398	82	130	22	15	14	79	.327	.378	.563	224
1885	27	BUF	NL	98	407	87	146	32	11	7	59	.359	.408	.543	221
1886	28	DTN	NL	121	489	139	181	40	15	11	72	.370	.445	.581	284
1887	29	DTN	NL	123	500	153	169	36	20	12	101	.338	.426	.562	281
1888	30	DTN	NL	129	522	118	160	33	11	9	66	.307	.399	.464	242
1889	31	BSN	NL	126	485	105	181	26	9	7	118	.373	.462	.507	246
1890	32	BOS	PL	123	460	117	152	36	9	1	97	.330	.466	.454	209
1891	33	BOS	AA	130	486	117	170	26	19	5	109	.350	.471	.512	249
1892	34	BRO	NL	152	588	121	197	30	20	5	124	.335	.432	.480	282
1893	35	BRO	NL	77	282	57	95	21	11	2	59	.337	.450	.511	144
1894	36	BLN	NL	123	525	137	182	39	23	9	128	.347	.425	.560	294
1895	37	BLN	NL	5	23	2	6	2	0	0	5	.261	.292	.348	8
		LOU	NL	24	97	13	30	10	1	2	15	.309	.380	.495	48
		TOT	NL	29	120	15	36	12	1	2	20	.300	.364	.467	56
1896	38	PHI	NL	57	218	42	75	13	3	1	41	.344	.462	.445	97
1904	46	NYG	NL	2	5	0	0	0	0	0	0	.000	.000	.000	0
Totals				1673	6711	1523	2296	460	205	106	1296	.342	.423	.519	3484

Orlando Cepeda

Bats: Right Throws: Right
Height: 6' 2" Weight: 210 lb.
Born: September 17, 1937 in Ponce,
Puerto Rico.
Hall of Fame Inductee — 1999

Transcendental Graphics

Year	Ag	Tm	Lg	G	AB	R	H	2B	3B	HR	RBI	BA	OBP	SLG	TB
1958	20	SFG	NL	148	603	88	188	38	4	25	96	.312	.342	.512	309
1959	21	SFG	NL	151	605	92	192	35	4	27	105	.317	.355	.522	316
1960	22	SFG	NL	151	569	81	169	36	3	24	96	.297	.343	.497	283
1961	23	SFG	NL	152	585	105	182	28	4	46	142	.311	.362	.609	356
1962	24	SFG	NL	162	625	105	191	26	1	35	114	.306	.347	.518	324
1963	25	SFG	NL	156	579	100	183	33	4	34	97	.316	.366	.563	326
1964	26	SFG	NL	142	529	75	161	27	2	31	97	.304	.361	.539	285
1965	27	SFG	NL	33	34	1	6	1	0	1	5	.176	.225	.294	10
1966	28	SFG	NL	19	49	5	14	2	0	3	15	.286	.352	.510	25
		STL	NL	123	452	65	137	24	0	17	58	.303	.362	.469	212
		TOT	NL	142	501	70	151	26	0	20	73	.301	.361	.473	237
1967	29	STL	NL	151	563	91	183	37	0	25	111	.325	.399	.524	295
1968	30	STL	NL	157	600	71	149	26	2	16	73	.248	.306	.378	227
1969	31	ATL	NL	154	573	74	147	28	2	22	88	.257	.325	.428	245
1970	32	ATL	NL	148	567	87	173	33	0	34	111	.305	.365	.543	308
1971	33	ATL	NL	71	250	31	69	10	1	14	44	.276	.330	.492	123
1972	34	ATL	NL	28	84	6	25	3	0	4	9	.298	.352	.476	40
		OAK	AL	3	3	0	0	0	0	0	0	.000	.000	.000	0
		TOT		31	87	6	25	3	0	4	9	.287	.340	.460	40
1973	35	BOS	AL	142	550	51	159	25	0	20	86	.289	.350	.444	244
1974	36	KCR	AL	33	107	3	23	5	0	1	18	.215	.282	.290	31
Totals				2124	7927	1131	2351	417	27	379	1365	.297	.350	.499	3959

Transcendental Graphics

Frank Chance

Bats: Right Throws: Right
Height: 6' 0" Weight: 190
Born: September 9, 1877 in Fresno, CA
Died: September 15, 1924 in Los Angeles, CA
Hall of Fame Inductee — 1946

Year	Ag	Tm	Lg	G	AB	R	H	2B	3B	HR	RBI	BA	OBP	SLG	TB
1898	20	CHC	NL	53	147	32	41	4	3	1	14	.279	.338	.367	54
1899	21	CHC	NL	64	192	37	55	6	2	1	22	.286	.351	.354	68
1900	22	CHC	NL	56	149	26	44	9	3	0	13	.295	.413	.396	59
1901	23	CHC	NL	69	241	38	67	12	4	0	36	.278	.376	.361	87
1902	24	CHC	NL	75	240	39	69	9	4	1	31	.288	.396	.371	89
1903	25	CHC	NL	125	441	83	144	24	0	2	81	.327	.439	.440	194
1904	26	CHC	NL	124	451	89	140	16	10	6	49	.310	.382	.430	194
1905	27	CHC	NL	118	392	92	124	16	12	2	70	.316	.450	.434	170
1906	28	CHC	NL	136	474	103	151	24	10	3	71	.319	.419	.430	204
1907	29	CHC	NL	111	382	58	112	19	2	1	49	.293	.395	.361	138
1908	30	CHC	NL	129	452	65	123	27	4	2	55	.272	.338	.363	164
1909	31	CHC	NL	93	324	53	88	16	4	0	46	.272	.341	.346	112
1910	32	CHC	NL	88	295	54	88	12	8	0	36	.298	.395	.393	116
1911	33	CHC	NL	31	88	23	21	6	3	1	17	.239	.432	.409	36
1912	34	CHC	NL	2	5	2	1	0	0	0	0	.200	.500	.200	1
1913	35	NYY	AL	12	24	3	5	0	0	0	6	.208	.406	.208	5
1914	36	NYY	AL	1	0	0	0	0	0	0	0	.000	.000	.000	0
Totals				1287	4297	797	1273	200	79	20	596	.296	.394	.394	1691

Roger Connor

Bats: Left Throws: Left
Height: 6' 3" Weight: 220 lb.
Born: July 1, 1857 in Waterbury, CT
Died: January 4, 1931 in Waterbury, CT
Hall of Fame Inductee — 1976

Transcendental Graphics

Year	Ag	Tm	Lg	G	AB	R	H	2B	3B	HR	RBI	BA	OBP	SLG	TB
1880	22	TRO	NL	83	340	53	113	18	8	3	47	.332	.357	.459	156
1881	23	TRO	NL	85	367	55	107	17	6	2	31	.292	.319	.387	142
1882	24	TRO	NL	81	349	65	115	22	18	4	42	.330	.354	.530	185
1883	25	NYG	NL	98	409	80	146	28	15	1	50	.357	.394	.506	207
1884	26	NYG	NL	116	477	98	151	28	4	4	82	.317	.367	.417	199
1885	27	NYG	NL	110	455	102	169	23	15	1	65	.371	.435	.495	225
1886	28	NYG	NL	118	485	105	172	29	20	7	71	.355	.405	.540	262
1887	29	NYG	NL	127	471	113	134	26	22	17	104	.285	.392	.541	255
1888	30	NYG	NL	134	481	98	140	15	17	14	71	.291	.389	.480	231
1889	31	NYG	NL	131	496	117	157	32	17	13	130	.317	.426	.528	262
1890	32	NYI	PL	123	484	133	169	24	15	14	103	.349	.450	.548	265
1891	33	NYG	NL	129	479	112	139	29	13	7	94	.290	.399	.449	215
1892	34	PHI	NL	155	564	123	166	37	11	12	73	.294	.420	.463	261
1893	35	NYG	NL	135	511	111	156	25	8	11	105	.305	.413	.450	230
1894	36	NYG	NL	22	82	10	24	7	0	1	14	.293	.356	.415	34
		STL	NL	99	380	83	122	28	25	7	79	.321	.410	.582	221
		TOT	NL	121	462	93	146	35	25	8	93	.316	.40	.552	255
1895	37	STL	NL	103	398	78	131	29	9	8	77	.329	.423	.508	202
1896	38	STL	NL	126	483	71	137	21	9	11	72	.284	.356	.433	209
1897	39	STL	NL	22	83	13	19	3	1	1	12	.229	.333	.325	27
Totals				**1997**	**7794**	**1620**	**2467**	**441**	**233**	**138**	**1322**	**.317**	**.397**	**.486**	**378**

Transcendental Graphics

Jimmie Foxx

Bats: Right Throws: Right
Height: 6' 0" Weight: 195 lb.
Born: October 22, 1907 in Sudlersville, MD
Died: July 21, 1967 in Miami, FL
Hall of Fame Inductee — 1951

Year	Ag	Tm	Lg	G	AB	R	H	2B	3B	HR	RBI	BA	OBP	SLG	TB
1925	17	PHA	AL	10	9	2	6	1	0	0	0	.667	.667	778	
1926	18	PHA	AL	26	32	8	10	2	1	0	5	.312	.333	.438	14
1927	19	PHA	AL	61	130	23	42	6	5	3	20	.323	.393	.515	67
1928	20	PHA	AL	118	400	85	131	29	10	13	79	.328	.416	.548	219
1929	21	PHA	AL	149	517	123	183	23	9	33	118	.354	.463	.625	323
1930	22	PHA	AL	153	562	127	188	33	13	37	156	.335	.429	.637	358
1931	23	PHA	AL	139	515	93	150	32	10	30	120	.291	.380	.567	292
1932	24	PHA	AL	154	585	151	213	33	9	58	169	.364	.469	.749	438
1933	25	PHA	AL	149	573	125	204	37	9	48	163	.356	.449	.703	403
1934	26	PHA	AL	150	539	120	180	28	6	44	130	.334	.449	.653	352
1935	27	PHA	AL	147	535	118	185	33	7	36	115	.346	.461	.636	340
1936	28	BOS	AL	155	585	130	198	32	8	41	143	.338	.440	.631	369
1937	29	BOS	AL	150	569	111	162	24	6	36	127	.285	.392	.538	306
1938	30	BOS	AL	149	565	139	197	33	9	50	175	.349	.462	.704	398
1939	31	BOS	AL	124	467	130	168	31	10	35	105	.360	.464	.694	324
1940	32	BOS	AL	144	515	106	153	30	4	36	119	.297	.412	.581	299
1941	33	BOS	AL	135	487	87	146	27	8	19	105	.300	.412	.505	246
1942	34	BOS	AL	30	100	18	27	4	0	5	14	.27	.39	.460	46
		CHC	NL	70	205	25	42	8	0	3	19	.205	.282	.288	59
		TOT		100	305	43	69	12	0		33	.22		.320	.344	105
1944	36	CHC	NL	15	20	0	1	1	0	0	2	.050	.136	.100	2
1945	37	PHI	NL	89	224	30	60	11	1	7	38	.268	.336	.420	94
Totals				2317	8134	1751	2646	458	125	534	1922	.325	.428	.609	4956

Lou Gehrig
Bats: Left Throws: Left
Height: 6' 0" Weight: 200 lb.
Born: June 19, 1903 in New York, NY
Died: June 2, 1941 in Riverdale, NY
Hall of Fame Inductee — 1939

Transcendental Graphics

Year	Ag	Tm	Lg	G	AB	R	H	2B	3B	HR	RBI	BA	OBP	SLG	TB
1923	20	NYY	AL	13	26	6	11	4	1	1	9	.423	.464	.769	20
1924	21	NYY	AL	10	12	2	6	1	0	0	5	.500	.538	.583	7
1925	22	NYY	AL	126	437	73	129	23	10	20	68	.295	.365	.531	232
1926	23	NYY	AL	155	572	135	179	47	20	16	112	.313	.420	.549	314
1927	24	NYY	AL	155	584	149	218	52	18	47	175	.373	.474	.765	447
1928	25	NYY	AL	154	562	139	210	47	13	27	142	.374	.467	.648	364
1929	26	NYY	AL	154	553	127	166	32	10	35	126	.300	.431	.584	323
1930	27	NYY	AL	154	581	143	220	42	17	41	174	.379	.473	.721	419
1931	28	NYY	AL	155	619	163	211	31	15	46	184	.341	.446	.662	410
1932	29	NYY	AL	156	596	138	208	42	9	34	151	.349	.451	.621	370
1933	30	NYY	AL	152	593	138	198	41	12	32	139	.334	.424	.605	359
1934	31	NYY	AL	154	579	128	210	40	6	49	165	.363	.465	.706	409
1935	32	NYY	AL	149	535	125	176	26	10	30	119	.329	.466	.583	312
1936	33	NYY	AL	155	579	167	205	37	7	49	152	.354	.478	.696	403
1937	34	NYY	AL	157	569	138	200	37	9	37	159	.351	.473	.643	366
1938	35	NYY	AL	157	576	115	170	32	6	29	114	.295	.410	.523	301
1939	36	NYY	AL	8	28	2	4	0	0	0	1	.143	.273	.143	4
Totals					2164	8001	1888	2721	534	163	493	1995	.340	.447	.632	5060

Hank Greenberg

Bats: Right Throws: Right
Height: 6' 0" Weight: 210 lb.
Born: January 1, 1911 in New York, NY
Died: September 4, 1986 in Beverly Hills, CA
Hall of Fame Inductee — 1956

Year	Ag	Tm	Lg	G	AB	R	H	2B	3B	HR	RBI	BA	OBP	SLG	TB
1930	19	DET	AL	1	1	0	0	0	0	0	0	.000	.000	.000	0
1933	22	DET	AL	117	449	59	135	33	3	12	87	.301	.367	.468	210
1934	23	DET	AL	153	593	118	201	63	7	26	139	.339	.404	.600	356
1935	24	DET	AL	152	619	121	203	46	16	36	170	.328	.411	.628	389
1936	25	DET	AL	12	46	10	16	6	2	1	16	.348	.455	.630	29
1937	26	DET	AL	154	594	137	200	49	14	40	183	.337	.436	.668	397
1938	27	DET	AL	155	556	144	175	23	4	58	146	.315	.438	.683	380
1939	28	DET	AL	138	500	112	156	42	7	33	112	.312	.420	.622	311
1940	29	DET	AL	148	573	129	195	50	8	41	150	.340	.433	.670	384
1941	30	DET	AL	19	67	12	18	5	1	2	12	.269	.410	.463	31
1945	34	DET	AL	78	270	47	84	20	2	13	60	.311	.404	.544	147
1946	35	DET	AL	142	523	91	145	29	5	44	127	.277	.373	.604	316
1947	36	PIT	NL	125	402	71	100	13	2	25	74	.249	.408	.478	192
Totals				**1394**	**5193**	**1051**	**1628**	**379**	**71**	**331**	**1276**	**.313**	**.412**	**.605**	**3142**

George Kelly

Bats: Right Throws: Right
Height: 6' 4" Weight 190 lb.
Born: September 10, 1895 in San Francisco, CA
Died: October 13, 1984 in Burlingame, CA
Hall of Fame Inductee — 1973

Transcendental Graphics

Year	Ag	Tm	Lg	G	AB	R	H	2B	3B	HR	RBI	BA	OBP	SLG	TB
1915	19	NYG	NL	17	38	2	6	0	0	1	4	.158	.179	.237	9
1916	20	NYG	NL	49	76	4	12	2	1	0	3	.158	.220	.211	16
1917	21	NYG	NL	11	7	0	0	0	0	0	0	.000	.000	.000	0
		PIT	NL	8	23	2	2	0	1	0	0	.087	.125	.174	4
		TOT	NL	19	30	2	2	0	1	0	0	.067	.097	.133	4
1919	23	NYG	NL	32	107	12	31	6	2	1	14	.290	.315	.411	44
1920	24	NYG	NL	155	590	69	157	22	11	11	94	.266	.320	.397	234
1921	25	NYG	NL	149	587	95	181	42	9	23	122	.308	.356	.528	310
1922	26	NYG	NL	151	592	96	194	33	8	17	107	.328	.363	.497	294
1923	27	NYG	NL	145	560	82	172	23	5	16	103	.307	.362	.452	253
1924	28	NYG	NL	144	571	91	185	37	9	21	136	.324	.371	.531	303
1925	29	NYG	NL	147	586	87	181	29	3	20	99	.309	.350	.471	276
1926	30	NYG	NL	136	499	70	151	24	4	13	80	.303	.352	.445	222
1927	31	CIN	NL	61	222	27	60	16	4	5	21	.270	.308	.446	99
1928	32	CIN	NL	116	402	46	119	33	7	3	58	.296	.345	.435	175
1929	33	CIN	NL	147	577	73	169	45	9	5	103	.293	.332	.428	247
1930	34	CIN	NL	51	188	18	54	10	1	5	35	.287	.313	.431	81
		CHC	NL	39	166	22	55	6	1	3	19	.331	.362	.434	72
		TOT	NL	90	354	40	109	16	2	8	54	.308	.336	.432	153
1932	36	BRO	NL	64	202	23	49	9	1	4	22	.243	.317	.356	72
Totals				**1622**	**5993**	**819**	**1778**	**337**	**76**	**148**	**1020**	**.297**	**.342**	**.452**	**2711**

Transcendental Graphics

Harmon Killebrew

Bats: Right Throws: Right
Height: 5' 11" Weight: 213 lb.
Born: June 29, 1936 in Payette, ID
Hall of Fame Inductee — 1984

Year	Ag	Tm	Lg	G	AB	R	H	2B	3B	HR	RBI	BA	OBP	SLG	TB
1954	18	WSH	AL	9	13	1	4	1	0	0	3	.308	.400	.385	5
1955	19	WSH	AL	38	80	12	16	1	0	4	7	.200	.281	.362	29
1956	20	WSH	AL	44	99	10	22	2	0	5	13	.222	.291	.394	39
1957	21	WSH	AL	9	31	4	9	2	0	2	5	.290	.333	.548	17
1958	22	WSH	AL	13	31	2	6	0	0	0	2	.194	.212	.194	6
1959	23	WSH	AL	153	546	98	132	20	2	42	105	.242	.354	.516	282
1960	24	WSH	AL	124	442	84	122	19	1	31	80	.276	.375	.534	236
1961	25	MIN	AL	150	541	94	156	20	7	46	122	.288	.405	.606	328
1962	26	MIN	AL	155	552	85	134	21	1	48	126	.243	.366	.545	301
1963	27	MIN	AL	142	515	88	133	18	0	45	96	.258	.349	.555	286
1964	28	MIN	AL	158	577	95	156	11	1	49	111	.270	.377	.548	316
1965	29	MIN	AL	113	401	78	108	16	1	25	75	.269	.384	.501	201
1966	30	MIN	AL	162	569	89	160	27	1	39	110	.281	.391	.538	306
1967	31	MIN	AL	163	547	105	147	24	1	44	113	.269	.408	.558	305
1968	32	MIN	AL	100	295	40	62	7	2	17	40	.210	.361	.420	124
1969	33	MIN	AL	162	555	106	153	20	2	49	140	.276	.427	.584	324
1970	34	MIN	AL	157	527	96	143	20	1	41	113	.271	.411	.546	288
1971	35	MIN	AL	147	500	61	127	19	1	28	119	.254	.386	.464	232
1972	36	MIN	AL	139	433	53	100	13	2	26	74	.231	.367	.450	195
1973	37	MIN	AL	69	248	29	60	9	1	5	32	.242	.352	.347	86
1974	38	MIN	AL	122	333	28	74	7	0	13	54	.222	.312	.360	120
1975	39	KCR	AL	106	312	25	62	13	0	14	44	.199	.317	.375	117
Totals					2435	8147	1283	2086	290	24	573	1584	.256	.376	.509	4143

Buck Leonard
Bats: Left Throws: Left
Height: 5' 10" Weight: 185 lb.
Born: September 8, 1907 in Rocky Mount, NC
Died: November 27, 1997 in Rocky Mount, NC
Hall of Fame Inductee — 1972

Transcendental Graphics

(NO STATISTICS AVAILABLE)

Transcendental Graphics

Willie McCovey

Bats: Left Throws: Left
Height: 6' 4" Weight: 210 lb.
Born: January 10, 1938 in Mobile, AL
Hall of Fame Inductee — 1986

Year	Ag	Tm	Lg	G	AB	R	H	2B	3B	HR	RBI	BA	OBP	SLG	TB
1959	21	SFG	NL	52	192	32	68	9	5	13	38	.354	.429	.656	126
1960	22	SFG	NL	101	260	37	62	15	3	13	51	.238	.349	.469	122
1961	23	SFG	NL	106	328	59	89	12	3	18	50	.271	.350	.491	161
1962	24	SFG	NL	91	229	41	67	6	1	20	54	.293	.368	.590	135
1963	25	SFG	NL	152	564	103	158	19	5	44	102	.280	.350	.566	319
1964	26	SFG	NL	130	364	55	80	14	1	18	54	.220	.336	.412	150
1965	27	SFG	NL	160	540	93	149	17	4	39	92	.276	.381	.539	291
1966	28	SFG	NL	150	502	85	148	26	6	36	96	.295	.391	.586	294
1967	29	SFG	NL	135	456	73	126	17	4	31	91	.276	.378	.535	244
1968	30	SFG	NL	148	523	81	153	16	4	36	105	.293	.378	.545	285
1969	31	SFG	NL	149	491	101	157	26	2	45	126	.320	.453	.656	322
1970	32	SFG	NL	152	495	98	143	39	2	39	126	.289	.444	.612	303
1971	33	SFG	NL	105	329	45	91	13	0	18	70	.277	.396	.480	158
1972	34	SFG	NL	81	263	30	56	8	0	14	35	.213	.316	.403	106
1973	35	SFG	NL	130	383	52	102	14	3	29	75	.266	.420	.546	209
1974	36	SDP	NL	128	344	53	87	19	1	22	63	.253	.416	.506	174
1975	37	SDP	NL	122	413	43	104	17	0	23	68	.252	.345	.460	190
1976	38	SDP	NL	71	202	20	41	9	0	7	36	.203	.281	.351	71
		OAK	AL	11	24	0	5	0	0	0	0	.208	.296	.208	5
		TOT		82	226	20	46	9	0	7	36	.204	.283	.336	76
1977	39	SFG	NL	141	478	54	134	21	0	28	86	.280	.367	.500	239
1978	40	SFG	NL	108	351	32	80	19	2	12	64	.228	.298	.396	139
1979	41	SFG	NL	117	353	34	88	9	0	15	57	.249	.318	.402	142
1980	42	SFG	NL	48	113	8	23	8	0	1	16	.204	.285	.301	34
Totals				2588	8197	1229	2211	353	46	521	1555	.270	.374	.515	4219

Johnny Mize

Bats: Left Throws: Right
Height 6' 2" Weight 215 lb.
Born: January 7, 1913 in Demorest, GA
Died: June 2, 1993 in Demorest, GA
Hall of Fame Inductee — 1981

Transcendental Graphics

Year	Ag	Tm	Lg	G	AB	R	H	2B	3B	HR	RBI	BA	OBP	SLG	TB
1936	23	STL	NL	126	414	76	136	30	8	19	93	.329	.402	.577	239
1937	24	STL	NL	145	560	103	204	40	7	25	113	.364	.427	.595	333
1938	25	STL	NL	149	531	85	179	34	16	27	102	.337	.422	.614	326
1939	26	STL	NL	153	564	104	197	44	14	28	108	.349	.444	.626	353
1940	27	STL	NL	155	579	111	182	31	13	43	137	.314	.404	.636	368
1941	28	STL	NL	126	473	67	150	39	8	16	100	.317	.406	.535	253
1942	29	NYG	NL	142	541	97	165	25	7	26	110	.305	.380	.521	282
1946	33	NYG	NL	101	377	70	127	18	3	22	70	.337	.437	.576	217
1947	34	NYG	NL	154	586	137	177	26	2	51	138	.302	.384	.614	360
1948	35	NYG	NL	152	560	110	162	26	4	40	125	.289	.395	.564	316
1949	36	NYG	NL	106	388	59	102	15	0	18	62	.263	.351	.441	171
		NYY	AL	13	23	4	6	1	0	1	2	.261	.393	.435	10
		TOT		119	411	63	108	16	0	19	64	.263	.354	.440	181
1950	37	NYY	AL	90	274	43	76	12	0	25	72	.277	.351	.595	163
1951	38	NYY	AL	113	332	37	86	14	1	10	49	.259	.339	.398	132
1952	39	NYY	AL	78	137	9	36	9	0	4	29	.263	.327	.416	57
1953	40	NYY	AL	81	104	6	26	3	0	4	27	.250	.339	.394	41
Totals				1884	6443	1118	2011	367	83	359	1337	**.312**	**.397**	**.562**	**3621**

Eddie Murray

Bats: Both Throws: Right
Height: 6' 2" Weight: 200 lb.
Born: February 24, 1956 in Los Angeles, CA
Hall of Fame Inductee — 2003

Transcendental Graphics

Year	Ag	Tm	Lg	G	AB	R	H	2B	3B	HR	RBI	BA	OBP	SLG	TB
1977	21	BAL	AL	160	611	81	173	29	2	27	88	.283	.333	.470	287
1978	22	BAL	AL	161	610	85	174	32	3	27	95	.285	.356	.480	293
1979	23	BAL	AL	159	606	90	179	30	2	25	99	.295	.369	.475	288
1980	24	BAL	AL	158	621	100	186	36	2	32	116	.300	.354	.519	322
1981	25	BAL	AL	99	378	57	111	21	2	22	78	.294	.360	.534	202
1982	26	BAL	AL	151	550	87	174	30	1	32	110	.316	.391	.549	302
1983	27	BAL	AL	156	582	115	178	30	3	33	111	.306	.393	.538	313
1984	28	BAL	AL	162	588	97	180	26	3	29	110	.306	.410	.509	299
1985	29	BAL	AL	156	583	111	173	37	1	31	124	.297	.383	.523	305
1986	30	BAL	AL	137	495	61	151	25	1	17	84	.305	.396	.463	229
1987	31	BAL	AL	160	618	89	171	28	3	30	91	.277	.352	.477	295
1988	32	BAL	AL	161	603	75	171	27	2	28	84	.284	.361	.474	286
1989	33	LAD	NL	160	594	66	147	29	1	20	88	.247	.342	.401	238
1990	34	LAD	NL	155	558	96	184	22	3	26	95	.330	.414	.520	290
1991	35	LAD	NL	153	576	69	150	23	1	19	96	.260	.321	.403	232
1992	36	NYM	NL	156	551	64	144	37	2	16	93	.261	.336	.423	233
1993	37	NYM	NL	154	610	77	174	28	1	27	100	.285	.325	.467	285
1994	38	CLE	AL	108	433	57	110	21	1	17	76	.254	.302	.425	184
1995	39	CLE	AL	113	436	68	141	21	0	21	82	.323	.375	.516	225
1996	40	CLE	AL	88	336	33	88	9	1	12	45	.262	.326	.402	135
		BAL	AL	64	230	36	59	12	0	10	34	.257	.327	.439	101
		TOT	AL	152	566	69	147	21	1	22	79	.260	.327	.417	236
1997	41	ANA	AL	46	160	13	35	7	0	3	15	.219	.273	.319	51
		LAD	NL	9	7	0	2	0	0	0	3	.286	.444	.286	2
		TOT		55	167	13	37	7	0	3	18	.222	.281	.317	53
Totals				3026	11336	1627	3255	504	35	504	1917	.287	.359	.476	5397

Tony Perez

Bats: Right Throws: Right
Height: 6' 2" Weight: 205 lb.
Born: May 14, 1942 in Ciego De Avila, Cuba
Hall of Fame Inductee — 2000

Transcendental Graphics

Year	Ag	Tm	Lg	G	AB	R	H	2B	3B	HR	RBI	BA	OBP	SLG	TB
1964	22	CIN	NL	12	25	1	2	1	0	0	1	.080	.179	.120	3
1965	23	CIN	NL	104	281	40	73	14	4	12	47	.260	.315	.466	131
1966	24	CIN	NL	99	257	25	68	10	4	4	39	.265	.304	.381	98
1967	25	CIN	NL	156	600	78	174	28	7	26	102	.290	.328	.490	294
1968	26	CIN	NL	160	625	93	176	25	7	18	92	.282	.338	.430	269
1969	27	CIN	NL	160	629	103	185	31	2	37	122	.294	.357	.526	331
1970	28	CIN	NL	158	587	107	186	28	6	40	129	.317	.401	.589	346
1971	29	CIN	NL	158	609	72	164	22	3	25	91	.269	.325	.438	267
1972	30	CIN	NL	136	515	64	146	33	7	21	90	.283	.349	.497	256
1973	31	CIN	NL	151	564	73	177	33	3	27	101	.314	.393	.527	297
1974	32	CIN	NL	158	596	81	158	28	2	28	101	.265	.331	.460	274
1975	33	CIN	NL	137	511	74	144	28	3	20	109	.282	.350	.466	238
1976	34	CIN	NL	139	527	77	137	32	6	19	91	.260	.328	.452	238
1977	35	MON	NL	154	559	71	158	32	6	19	91	.283	.352	.463	259
1978	36	MON	NL	148	544	63	158	38	3	14	78	.290	.336	.449	244
1979	37	MON	NL	132	489	58	132	29	4	13	73	.270	.322	.425	208
1980	38	BOS	AL	151	585	73	161	31	3	25	105	.275	.320	.467	273
1981	39	BOS	AL	84	306	35	77	11	3	9	39	.252	.310	.395	121
1982	40	BOS	AL	69	196	18	51	14	2	6	31	.260	.326	.444	87
1983	41	PHI	NL	91	253	18	61	11	2	6	43	.241	.316	.372	94
1984	42	CIN	NL	71	137	9	33	6	1	2	15	.241	.295	.343	47
1985	43	CIN	NL	72	183	25	60	8	0	6	33	.328	.396	.470	86
1986	44	CIN	NL	77	200	14	51	12	1	2	29	.255	.333	.355	71
Totals					2777	9778	1272	2732	505	79	379	1652	.279	.341	.463	4532

167

Transcendental Graphics

George Sisler

Bats: Left Throws: Left
Height: 5' 11" Weight: 170 lb.
Born: March 24, 1893 in Manchester, OH
Died: March 26, 1973 in Richmond Heights, MO
Hall of Fame Inductee —1939

Year	Ag	Tm	Lg	G	AB	R	H	2B	3B	HR	RBI	BA	OBP	SLG	TB
1915	22	SLB	AL	81	274	28	78	10	2	3	29	.285	.307	.369	101
1916	23	SLB	AL	151	580	83	177	21	11	4	76	.305	.355	.400	232
1917	24	SLB	AL	135	539	60	190	30	9	2	52	.353	.390	.453	244
1918	25	SLB	AL	114	452	69	154	21	9	2	41	.341	.400	.440	199
1919	26	SLB	AL	132	511	96	180	31	15	10	83	.352	.390	.530	271
1920	27	SLB	AL	154	631	137	257	49	18	19	122	.407	.449	.632	399
1921	28	SLB	AL	138	582	125	216	38	18	12	104	.371	.411	.560	326
1922	29	SLB	AL	142	586	134	246	42	18	8	105	.420	.467	.594	348
1924	31	SLB	AL	151	636	94	194	27	10	9	74	.305	.340	.421	268
1925	32	SLB	AL	150	649	100	224	21	15	12	105	.345	.371	.479	311
1926	33	SLB	AL	150	613	78	178	21	12	7	71	.290	.327	.398	244
1927	34	SLB	AL	149	614	87	201	32	8	5	97	.327	.357	.430	264
1928	35	WSH	AL	20	49	1	12	1	0	0	2	.245	.260	.265	13
		BSN	NL	118	491	71	167	26	4	4	68	.340	.380	.434	213
		TOT		138	540	72	179	27	4	4	70	.331	.370	.419	226
1929	36	BSN	NL	154	629	67	205	40	8	2	79	.326	.363	.424	267
1930	37	BSN	NL	116	431	54	133	15	7	3	67	.309	.346	.397	171
Totals				**2055**	**8267**	**1284**	**2812**	**425**	**164**	**102**	**1175**	**.340**	**.379**	**.468**	**3871**

Bill Terry

Bats: Left Throws: Left
Height: 6' 1" Weight: 200 lb.
Born: October 30, 1898 in Atlanta, GA
Died: January 9, 1989 in Jacksonville, FL
Hall of Fame Inductee — 1954

Year	Ag	Tm	Lg	G	AB	R	H	2B	3B	HR	RBI	BA	OBP	SLG	TB
1923	24	NYG	NL	3	7	1	1	0	0	0	0	.143	.333	.143	1
1924	25	NYG	NL	77	163	26	39	7	2	5	24	.239	.311	.399	65
1925	26	NYG	NL	133	489	75	156	31	6	11	70	.319	.374	.474	232
1926	27	NYG	NL	98	225	26	65	12	5	5	43	.289	.352	.453	102
1927	28	NYG	NL	150	580	101	189	32	13	20	121	.326	.377	.529	307
1928	29	NYG	NL	149	568	100	185	36	11	17	101	.326	.394	.518	294
1929	30	NYG	NL	150	607	103	226	39	5	14	117	.372	.418	.522	317
1930	31	NYG	NL	154	633	139	254	39	15	23	129	.401	.452	.619	392
1931	32	NYG	NL	153	611	121	213	43	20	9	112	.349	.397	.529	323
1932	33	NYG	NL	154	643	124	225	42	11	28	117	.350	.382	.580	373
1933	34	NYG	NL	123	475	68	153	20	5	6	58	.322	.375	.423	201
1934	35	NYG	NL	153	602	109	213	30	6	8	83	.354	.414	.463	279
1935	36	NYG	NL	145	596	91	203	32	8	6	64	.341	.383	.451	269
1936	37	NYG	NL	79	229	36	71	10	5	2	39	.310	.363	.424	97
Totals				**1721**	**6428**	**1120**	**2193**	**373**	**112**	**154**	**1078**	**.341**	**.393**	**.506**	**3252**

Gold Glove First Basemen

The Gold Glove Award was first presented by Rawlings in 1957 to honor the nine best fielders in each league at their respective positions. The award is determined by a vote of managers and coaches from each major league team who are not eligible to vote for their own players.

National League	American League
1957	
Gil Hodges (Brooklyn)	
1958	
Gil Hodges (Los Angeles)	Vic Power (Cleveland)
1959	
Gil Hodges (Los Angeles)	Vic Power (Cleveland)
1960	
Bill White (St. Louis)	Vic Power (Cleveland)
1961	
Bill White (St. Louis)	Vic Power (Cleveland)
1962	
Bill White (St. Louis)	Vic Power (Minnesota)
1963	
Bill White (St. Louis)	Vic Power (Minnesota)
1964	
Bill White (St. Louis)	Vic Power (Minnesota)
1965	
Bill White (St. Louis)	Joe Pepitone (New York)
1966	
Bill White (Philadelphia)	Joe Pepitone (New York)

1967
Wes Parker (Los Angeles)   George Scott (Boston)

1968
Wes Parker (Los Angeles)   George Scott (Boston)

1969
Wes Parker (Los Angeles)   Joe Pepitone (New York)

1970
Wes Parker (Los Angeles)   Jim Spencer (California)

1971
Wes Parker (Los Angeles)   George Scott (Boston)

1972
Wes Parker (Los Angeles)   George Scott (Milwaukee)

1973
Mike Jorgensen (Montreal)   George Scott (Milwaukee)

1974
Steve Garvey (Los Angeles) George Scott (Milwaukee)

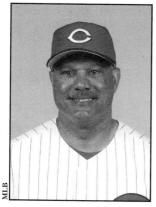

CHRIS CHAMBLISS

CECIL COOPER

1975
Steve Garvey (Los Angeles)   George Scott (Milwaukee)

1976
Steve Garvey (Los Angeles)   George Scott (Milwaukee)

1977
Steve Garvey (Los Angeles)   Jim Spencer (Chicago)

1978
Keith Hernandez (St. Louis)   Chris Chambliss (New York)

1979
Keith Hernandez (St. Louis)   Cecil Cooper (Milwaukee)

1980
Keith Hernandez (St. Louis)   Cecil Cooper (Milwaukee)

1981
Keith Hernandez (St. Louis/NY)   Mike Squires (Chicago)

1982
Keith Hernandez (New York)   Eddie Murray (Baltimore)

1983
Keith Hernandez (New York)   Eddie Murray (Baltimore)

1984
Keith Hernandez (New York)   Eddie Murray (Baltimore)

1985
Keith Hernandez (New York)   Don Mattingly (New York)

1986
Keith Hernandez (New York)   Don Mattingly (New York)

1987
Keith Hernandez (New York)   Don Mattingly (New York)

1988
Keith Hernandez (New York)   Don Mattingly (New York)

1989
Andres Galarraga (Montreal)   Don Mattingly (New York)
1990
Andres Galarraga (Montreal)   Mark McGwire (Oakland)
1991
Will Clark (San Francisco)   Don Mattingly (New York)
1992
Mark Grace (Chicago)   Don Mattingly (New York)
1993
Mark Grace (Chicago)   Don Mattingly (New York)
1994
Jeff Bagwell (Houston)   Don Mattingly (New York)
1995
Mark Grace (Chicago)   J.T. Snow (California)
1996
Mark Grace (Chicago)   J.T. Snow (California)
1997
J.T. Snow (San Francisco)   Rafael Palmeiro (Baltimore)
1998
J.T. Snow (San Francisco)   Rafael Palmeiro (Baltimore)
1999
J.T. Snow (San Francisco)   Rafael Palmeiro (Texas)
2000
J.T. Snow (San Francisco)   John Olerud (Seattle)
2001
Todd Helton (Colorado)   Doug Mientkiewicz (Minnesota)
2002
Todd Helton (Colorado)   John Olerud (Seattle)

2003
Derrek Lee (Chicago)   John Olerud (Seattle)

2004
Todd Helton (Colorado)   Darin Erstad (Anaheim)

2005
Derrek Lee (Chicago)   Mark Teixeira (Texas)

DARIN ERSTAD

MARK TEIXEIRA

Most Valuable Player — 1st Basemen

Year	Name	League	Team
1932	Jimmie Foxx	American	Philadelphia
1933	Jimmie Foxx	American	Philadelphia
1935	Hank Greenberg	American	Detroit
1936	Lou Gehrig	American	New York
1938	Jimmie Foxx	American	Boston
1940	Frank McCormick	National	Cincinnati
1941	Dolph Camili	National	Brooklyn
1945	Phil Cavaretta	National	Chicago
1946	Stan Musial	National	St. Louis
1967	Orlando Cepeda	National	St. Louis
1969	Willie McCovey	National	San Francisco
1970	Boog Powell	American	Baltimore
1972	Dick Allen	American	Chicago
1974	Steve Garvey	National	Los Angeles
1977	Rod Carew	American	Minnesota
1979	Willie Stargell	National	Pittsburgh
1979	Keith Hernandez	National	St. Louis

ALBERT PUJOLS

1985	Don Mattingly	American	New York
1993	Frank Thomas	American	Chicago
1994	Jeff Bagwell	National	Houston
1994	Frank Thomas	American	Chicago
1995	Mo Vaughn	American	Boston
2000	Jason Giambi	American	Oakland
2005	Albert Pujols	National	St. Louis

Rookie of the Year

Year	Name	Team
1947	Jackie Robinson	Brooklyn
1957	Ed Bouchee	Philadelphia
1958	Orlando Cepeda	San Francisco
1959	Willie McCovey	San Francisco
1967	Lee May	Cincinnati
1971	Chris Chambliss	Cleveland
1974	Mike Hargrove	Texas
1979	Pat Putnam	Texas
1984	Alvin Davis	Seattle
1987	Mark McGwire	Oakland
1988	Mark Grace	Chicago
1991	Jeff Bagwell	Houston
1992	Eric Karros	Los Angeles
1998	Todd Helton	Colorado
2005	Ryan Howard	Philadelphia

RYAN HOWARD

JEFF BAGWELL

Retired Numbers of 1st Basemen

Name	Team	Number
Harmon Killebrew	Minnesota	3
Lou Gehrig	New York	4
Hank Greenberg	Detroit	5
Steve Garvey	San Diego	6
Stan Musial	St. Louis	6
Willie Stargell	Pittsburgh	8
Don Mattingly	New York	23
Tony Perez	Cincinnati	24
Rod Carew	Minnesota	29
Rod Carew	Anaheim	29
Orlando Cepeda	San Francisco	30
Eddie Murray	Baltimore	33
Willie McCovey	San Francisco	44

Silver Slugger Award First Base

American League	National League
1980	
Cecil Cooper (Milwaukee)	Keith Hernandez (St. Louis)
1981	
Cecil Cooper (Milwaukee)	Pete Rose (Philadelphia)
1982	
Cecil Cooper (Milwaukee)	Al Oliver (Montreal)
1983	
Eddie Murray (Baltimore)	George Hendrick (St. Louis)
1984	
Eddie Murray (Baltimore)	Keith Hernandez (New York)
1985	
Don Mattingly (New York)	Jack Clark (St. Louis)
1986	
Don Mattingly (New York)	Glenn Davis (Houston)
1987	
Don Mattingly (New York)	Jack Clark (St. Louis)
1988	
George Brett (Kansas City)	Andres Galarraga (Montreal)
1989	
Fred McGriff (Toronto)	Will Clark (San Francisco)
1990	
Cecil Fielder (Detroit)	Eddie Murray (Los Angeles)
1991	
Cecil Fielder (Detroit)	Will Clark (San Francisco)
1992	
Mark McGwire (Oakland)	Fred McGriff (San Diego)

1993
Frank Thomas (Chicago)   Fred McGriff (Atlanta)

1994
Frank Thomas (Chicago)   Jeff Bagwell (Houston)

1995
Mo Vaughn (Boston)   Eric Karros (Los Angeles)

1996
Mark McGwire (Oakland)   Andres Galarraga (Colorado)

1997
Tino Martinez (New York)   Jeff Bagwell (Houston)

1998
Rafael Palmeiro (Baltimore)   Mark McGwire (St. Louis)

1999
Carlos Delgado (Toronto)   Jeff Bagwell (Houston)

CARLOS DELGADO

JASON GIAMBI

2000
Carlos Delgado (Toronto)   Todd Helton (Colorado)

2001
Jason Giambi (Oakland)   Todd Helton (Colorado)

2002
Jason Giambi (New York)   Todd Helton (Colorado)

2003
Carlos Delgado (Toronto)   Todd Helton (Colorado)

2004
Mark Teixeira (Texas)   Albert Pujols (St. Louis)

2005
Mark Teixeira (Texas)   Derrek Lee (Chicago)

The Lou Gehrig Memorial Award

Baseball fans voted Lou Gehrig of the New York Yankees the best first baseman of the 20th Century, but he was known for more than his prowess at the plate and in the field. Gehrig personified the gifted yet humble athlete who gave of himself to help others. In his honor, the Phi Delta Theta International Fraternity—to which he belonged as a student at Columbia University—created the Lou Gehrig Memorial Award "to recognize the Major League Baseball Player who best exemplifies the spirit and character of Lou Gehrig both on and off the field. The award was created to acknowledge an individual player's outstanding commitment to his community and philanthropy." A plaque containing the name of each winner since the award's creation in 1955 is located in the Baseball Hall of Fame and Museum in Cooperstown, New York. The following twelve first basemen have won the award (and it's probably no coincidence that more first basemen have won it than players at any other defensive position).

1957
Stan Musial - St. Louis Cardinals

1959
Gil Hodges - Los Angeles Dodgers

1967
Ernie Banks - Chicago Cubs

1971
Harmon Killebrew - Minnesota Twins

1972
Wes Parker - Los Angeles Dodgers

1980
Tony Perez - Boston Red Sox

1984
Steve Garvey - San Diego Padres

1990
Glenn Davis - Houston Astros

1991
Kent Hrbek - Minnesota Twins

1993
Don Mattingly - New York Yankees

1999
Mark McGwire - St. Louis Cardinals

2004
Jim Thome - Philadelphia Phillies

About the Author

Tom Keegan, a Hall of Fame voter, is the sports editor of the *Lawrence Journal-World*. He co-authored *Sleeper Cars and Flannel Uniforms* (Triumph Books, 2001) with Elden Auker and was sole author of *Ernie Harwell: My 60 Years in Baseball* (Triumph Books, 2002). Keegan, a 1981 graduate of Marquette University, covered the Dodgers for the *Orange County Register*, the Cubs for the *National Sports Daily*, the Orioles for the *Baltimore Sun*, and wrote a baseball column for the *New York Post*. He co-hosted a radio show for 1050 ESPN Radio in New York City for two-and-a-half years. Tom was honored as Communicator of the Year at Marquette University's 2005 Alumni Awards. He lives with his wife and family in Lawrence, Kansas.

Books of Interest

Baseball Behind the Seams

Each book in this one-of-a-kind series focuses on a single position, exploring it with the kind of depth serious fans crave. Through extensive research, including interviews with hundreds of players past and present, the authors have brought together the most original and informative series ever published on the game.

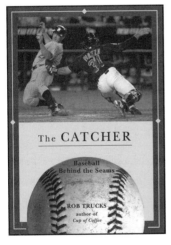

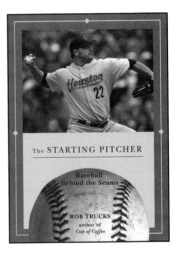

The Catcher
By Rob Trucks
$14.99 Paperback
1-57860-164-9

The Starting Pitcher
By Rob Trucks
$14.99 Paperback
1-57860-163-0

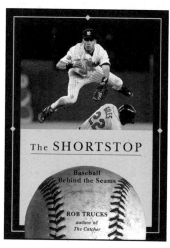

The Shortstop
By Rob Trucks
$14.95 Paperback
1-57860-262-9

Each book in the series covers

- The physical and mental qualities of the position
- The position's history
- The plays, and how to make them
- Profiles of the position's top all-time players
- The best defenders of the position
- A day in the life of one player, from arriving at the ballpark to the final out
- Lists of Gold Glovers, MVPs, and Rookies of the Year
- Fun and quirky facts about the position

Books of Interest

The Baseball Journal series

Each **Baseball Journal** book is organized by decade starting with the very first year of the team's history and continuing through the present. Team and player statistics and highlights of great games bring the numbers to life. Every year is given extensive coverage, from a statistical overview to a day-by-day breakdown. Each date in a team's history includes anecdotes, hitting and pitching highlights, plus interesting and unusual facts—much more than just a box score.

For baseball fans, the **Baseball Journal** series provides the opportunity to relive great plays, settle those "friendly wagers" and dive headfirst into the most fascinating, fact-filled book ever written on their favorite teams.

Cubs Journal
Year by Year & Day by Day
with the Chicago Cubs Since 1876

By John Snyder
Paperback $29.95
1-57860-192-4

"Every dedicated Cubs fan will want their very own copy of John Snyder's Cubs Journal!"
– *Midwest Book Review*

"Rating: Home Run"
– *Cubs Vineline*

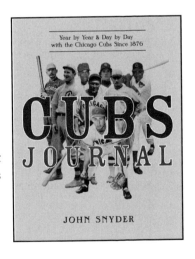

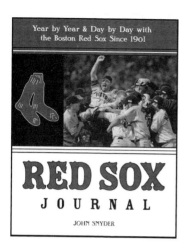

Red Sox Journal
Year by Year & Day by Day with the Boston Red Sox Since 1901

By John Snyder
Paperback $29.95
1-57860-253-X

The must-have guide for diehard Red Sox fans

Cardinals Journal
Year by Year & Day by Day with the St. Louis Cardinals Since 1882

By John Snyder
Paperback $29.95
1-57860-254-8

The definitive chronicle of one of Major League Baseball's most beloved franchises

Books of Interest

Red Legs and Black Sox
Edd Roush and the Untold Story of the 1919 World Series

By Susan Dellinger
Paperback $16.95
1-57860-229-7

"This is a book that should have been published a long time ago. The author gives a fresh look at the 1919 World Series through the eyes of the city of Cincinnati and the star of the Reds."
- *Bob Feller, Hall of Fame Pitcher for the Cleveland Indians*

"What a terrific saga."
- *William A. Cook, Author of* The 1919 World Series: What Really Happened

"I couldn't put it down! Susan Dellinger has expanded our knowledge of the events of 1919 and what actually went down on the diamond."
- *Robert H. Schaefer, 3-Time Winner of the McFarland-SABR Best Baseball Research Award*

All self-respecting baseball fans are familiar with the 1919 World Series between the Cincinnati Reds and the Chicago White Sox, in which eight members of the White Sox were banned from baseball for intentionally losing several games in that series. But there is another side to the story, revealed for the first time in *Red Legs and Black Sox.*

The star of the 1919 Reds was center fielder Edd Roush, who was later elected to the Baseball Hall of Fame. Roush's granddaughter, author Susan Dellinger, presents the Cincinnati Reds' perspective on this infamous event through research, historical documents, and most importantly, Roush's own words on the subject. This is a story that is far more complicated than previous movies and books have alluded to, involving fixes on both teams— and corruption right down to the leagues themselves.

Books of Interest

The Baseball Uncyclopedia:
A Highly Opinionated, Myth-Busting Guide to the Great American Game

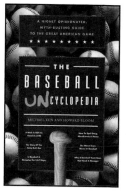

By Micheal Kun and
Howard Bloom
Paperback $14.95
1-57860-233-5

"Incredibly funny and so easy to relate to. A baseball book that reminds us it's just a game in the much bigger game of life."
—*Karl Ravech, Host, ESPN's* Baseball Tonight

The Baseball Uncyclopedia reveals the truth about the tall tales, ill-formed opinions, and widely held misunderstandings that baseball fans have clung to for generations.

Michael Kun and Howard Bloom explain that, contrary to popular belief, an American League team is *not* required to use a designated hitter. They argue that it's *not* always wrong to root against the home team. They heap scorn upon those who believe Joe DiMaggio was *ever* "The Greatest Living Baseball Player." They also offer tips on appropriate ballpark heckling and issue a condemnation of the writer responsible for Reggie Jackson's *Love Boat* appearance. And they reveal shocking information about Moises Alou's personal habits that will dismay even the most jaded baseball devotee.

Packed with surprising baseball facts as well as the musings of two baseball fanatics, crammed almost to bursting with argument starters, bet settlers, and absurd pop-culture references, **The Baseball Uncyclopedia** offers a sound rebuke to anyone who thinks a baseball book can't be smart, funny, and informative all at the same time.